MYTH, IDENTITY, AND SUBALTERNITY

A COMPARATIVE STUDY OF EUGENE O'NEILL AND GIRISH KARNAD

DR. PRIYANKA REDHU, DR. KANU PRIYA

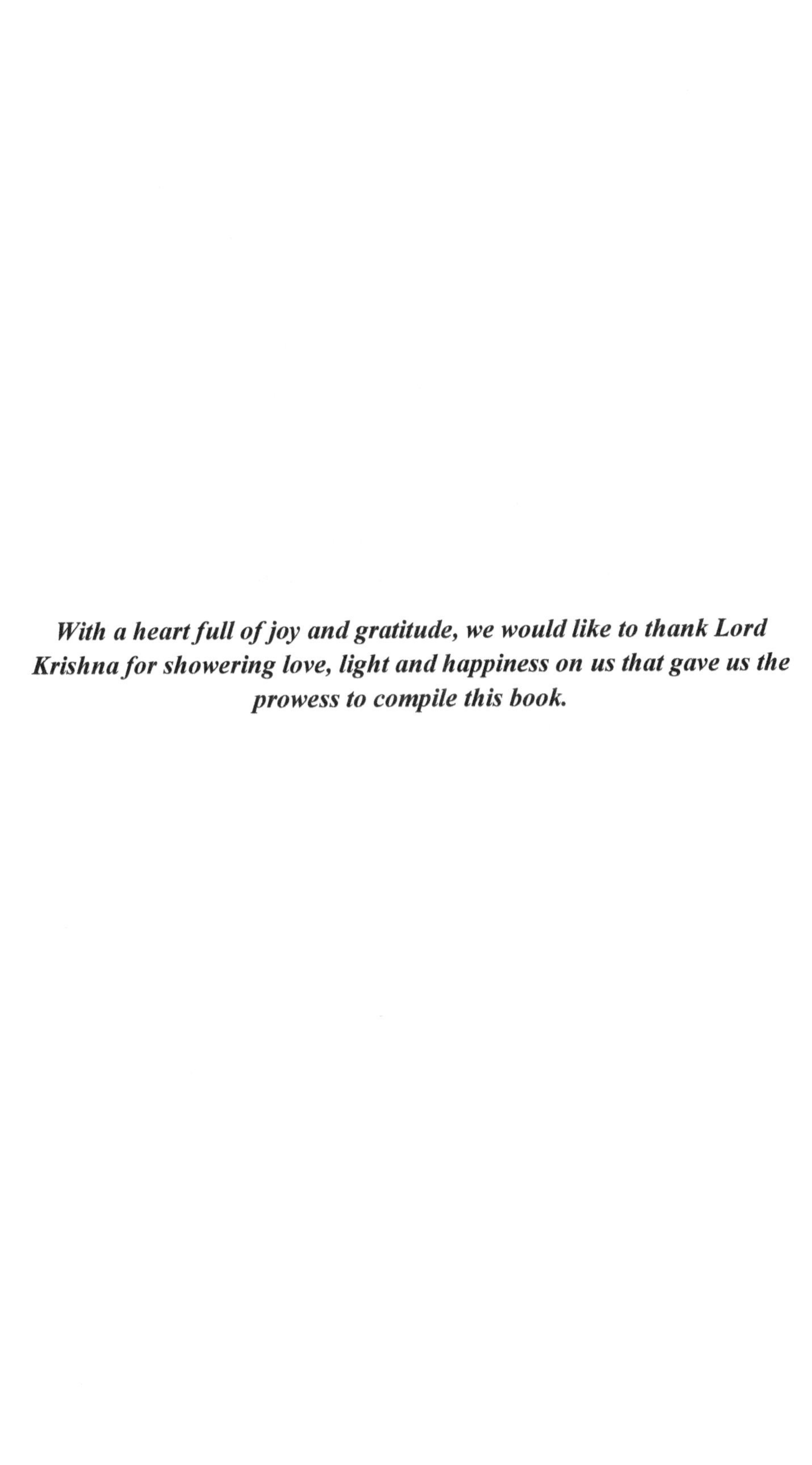

With a heart full of joy and gratitude, we would like to thank Lord Krishna for showering love, light and happiness on us that gave us the prowess to compile this book.

Contents

Acknowledgments

We hope this book not only provides an insight into a great world of possibilities and avenues to explore but also makes the readers relish as well as appreciate this work as scholarly research on Eugene O'Neill and Girish Karnad.

I, Dr. Priyanka Redhu, would like, first of all, to offer my heartfelt gratitude to my parents who had unflinching trust in me for completing this mammoth task and propelling me on each day to successfully finish my task. My heartfelt gratitude to my mother-in-law for her support and patience. I would also like

to thank the light of my life my grandmother Mrs. Pataso Devi for her positivity and inspiration and my late Grandfather Mr. Karanbir Singh Redhu along with my late uncles Mr. Rajbir Redhu and Mr. Hawa Singh Sheokand for silently showering their blessings on me.

I am highly and eternally grateful to the most important person in my life: My husband Mr. Anurag Gehlot for being my sounding board and encouraging me with his positivity and honest reviews.

I, Dr. Kanu Priya, warmly acknowledge and appreciate the unconditional inspiration and motivation I received from my parents, brother and sister. I would like to thank my husband Nitin for his unflinching support and confidence in me. I would like to convey my sincere thanks to all of them for reposing faith in me and allowing me to fulfil my dreams and their expectations. It is because of their efforts and encouragement that I have a legacy to pass on to my family where one didn't exist before.

This book is an outcome of our unending efforts and hard work and we hope that it opens avenues for further researches and keep us inspired to continue working with the same stride.

Dr. Priyanka Redhu

Dr. Kanu Priya

Introduction

Literature gives vent to an individual's feelings, ideas, and emotions. The writers navigate an individual's mind to the unheard and unseen, where language is only a form of expression. Reading these works of literature not only makes one reflect upon life but also comprehend background and milieu of the writer. Writers sketch their characters in order to make them an enigmatic literary subject. This has become a major area of study that has baffled and intrigued scholars and writers since time immemorial, starting with the Greeks to the writers of present times.

Drama is a manifestation of anticipation, aspirations, inside yearnings, achievements and dilemma of its people which is highly absorbing and entertaining as it represents action on stage. The word "drama" has its source in Greek. It originated from word "dra" meaning "do" (*Encyclopaedia* 1). In this way, "doing" or "action" is column beam of the whole dramatic premise. Aristotle, the Greek philosopher has also acknowledged action as the predominating component of drama. As compared to fiction where the narrative style and technique hold a significant position drama considers dialogue and action to be supreme. Literary critic and historian Compton- Rickett defines drama as a story represented in action (89).

Drama is an audible and visual narrative that is mimetic in nature as it represents a make-believe world and showcases characters in a fictional setting. Marjorie Boulton, British author and writer, has observed that a play is meant to be acted and has three dimensions. These three dimensions are sound, action and the act of seeing the play being performed. A true play is three-dimensional (3).

European drama originated from Greek drama. Ancient European drama was based on Greek myths until the establishment of Christianity which prohibited worshipping of Olympian Gods. This changed the themes of drama and included the ones which were inspired by everyday life. European drama made a very strong distinction of tragedies and comedies up until the arrival of Shakespeare and the 'University Wits' who gave rise to tragic-comedies that is a play that has a mix of tragic and comic features. This was done to refabricate the themes of European drama.

Earlier European dramas, which were based on myths, were narrated by the chorus when one day Aeschylus the great Greek dramatist called one of the chorus actors and made him converse with the team thus creating the first drama on stage. Aeschylus increased the possibility of dialogue and dramatic tension and allowed freedom of plot construction (Britannica 1).

Indian literature has its theory of drama, which is over two thousand years old, known as *The Natyashastra* that is written by Bharatamuni. In this ancient classical literature, drama was considered as "the fifth *Veda*" and it was pertinently designated as "*Drishya Kaayva*". Bharatamuni himself has explained the summary of his dramatic theory in the sixth chapter of his book *The Natyashastra* which is quoted by A.B.Keith in his book *The Sanskrit Drama*, " The combination called *natya* is a mixture of *rasa, bhavas, vrittis, pravrittis, siddhi, svaros, abhinayas, dharm* alongwith instruments, song and theatre – house"(12). It has taken words from *Rigveda*, melody from *Samaveda*, gestures from *Yajurveda* and emotions from *Atharvaveda*.

Indian drama has a very ancient history which is prominently influenced by Sanskrit literature. It structures around a *Nayak* (Hero), *Nayika* (heroine) and a Clown. Bharatamuni is called the Father of Indian Drama. In his great treatise *The Natyashashtra* while explaining the importance of theatre, he proclaims it to be an embodiment of life. All kinds of life, craft, learning and action finds its place in theatre (Ghosh 13).

Sanskrit dramas were popular until the fifteenth century and enacted in the cities of Tamil Nadu, Kerala, Karnataka, Andhra Pradesh, Uttar Pradesh and Gujarat. When the Indian continent suffered from invasion by various invaders it affected Indian drama as the theme changed from

Sanskrit folklores to regional folklores. Invasions were instrumental in popularizing regional dramas of various states and *Nautanki, Yatra, Ramlila* and various other forms of regional drama came into existence. After Indian Independence there was a significant change in the growth of drama which made it function in two styles; professional theatre and non- professional theatre.

This brief study of European and Indian drama shows that drama irrespective of time, place or milieu acts as a looking glass for the society. All kinds of dramas have a history of using ancient myths as one of their themes along with the eternal quest to find the self. The subjugation of the subalterns has also been an important theme. These themes prepared a common ground for researching the two great dramatists Eugene O' Neill and Girish Karnad as they have used similar theories and themes in their work of art as both were pioneers in representing human predicament.

An all-encompassing critical concept of cultural theory emerged in the latter half of twentieth century which included politics, history and ideology. This formed an independent genre of research which considered the parameters of cultural formation as the base of academic endeavour. This Cultural theory not only includes theoretical aspect but is also an academic introspection critiquing both classical and contemporary theories. Cultural studies consider all texts to be cultural constructs which an author reconstructs from his cultural space. It encompasses not only identity and its representation but gender, sexuality, subalternity, mythical perspective also plays a pivotal role.

The works by both writers look beyond the aesthetic parameters and address issues of social and cultural relevance. Their works critique culture and thereby make cultural criticism an inevitable part of literary creation in the present times. This makes both the writers, although separated by a long-time frame but known for their path breaking plays, as great subjects under the light of myths, quest for identity and subalternity.

The exploration of myths, the construction of identities, and the representation of subaltern voices within the realm of theatre have long been recognized as essential in shedding light on the intricate complexities of human existence. Theatre, as an art form, possesses the unique ability to reflect and challenge societal norms, unravelling the multidimensional layers of cultural, historical, and socio-political dynamics. This thesis aims to conduct a comparative study of two influential playwrights, Eugene O'Neill and Girish Karnad, in order to delve into the themes of myth, identity, and subalternity.

Eugene O'Neill, an eminent figure in American theatre, and Girish Karnad, a legendary playwright from India, may seemingly belong to distinct cultural and literary traditions. However, both O'Neill and Karnad share a common inclination towards exploring the complexities of human experiences and engaging with questions of identity and power. By analyzing their plays through the lenses of myth, identity, and subalternity, this thesis aims to highlight the shared concerns and distinctive approaches employed by these two playwrights.

Myth, as a potent narrative tool, plays a significant role in the works of both O'Neill and Karnad. They skilfully incorporate myths and legends to delve into the collective unconscious, unravelling deep-seated cultural and historical motifs that resonate within their respective societies. This study seeks to explore how O'Neill and Karnad utilize mythic elements in their plays and examines the impact of these narratives on the construction and portrayal of identity. Additionally, it aims to investigate the ways in which the playwrights navigate the complexities of power dynamics, shedding light on the marginalization and agency of subaltern characters within their respective social contexts.

Identity emerges as a central theme in this comparative study, as both O'Neill and Karnad grapple with questions of individual and collective identities in their works. Through their characters, they delve into existential crises arising from societal pressures, cultural conflicts, and personal struggles, probing the intricate dimensions of human identity. By analyzing their treatment of identity, this research aims to uncover how O'Neill and Karnad challenge dominant narratives, revealing the multiplicity and fluidity of human identities.

Moreover, the study delves into the representation of subaltern voices in the plays of O'Neill and Karnad. The concept of the subaltern, originally introduced by Antonio Gramsci, refers to marginalized and oppressed groups in society whose voices are often suppressed or disregarded. According to Gayatri Chakravorty Spivak, a prominent postcolonial theorist, "The subaltern refers to those individuals or groups who are socially, politically, and economically marginalized and whose voices are often silenced or ignored within dominant discourses" (Spivak 271). By examining the portrayal of subaltern characters in the works of these playwrights, this thesis seeks to shed light on the manner in which O'Neill and Karnad give agency and visibility to those historically silenced, providing a platform for their stories, struggles, and aspirations

Through a comparative analysis of the works of Eugene O'Neill and Girish Karnad, this book aims to uncover the intricate interplay between myth, identity, and subalternity within their respective dramatic landscapes. It endeavours to deepen our understanding of how theatre can challenge existing power structures, deconstruct dominant narratives, and pave the way for a more inclusive and empathetic society. By engaging with their plays, we can appreciate the transformative potential of theatre in transcending boundaries and cultures, uncovering universal.

EUGENE O' NEILL: BIOGRAPHY AND WRITING STYLE

Eugene O' Neill was born on October 16, 1865 in a hotel room of New York City. His father, James O'Neill, was a highly acclaimed theatre actor and mother Mary Ellen Quinlan, modest and naïve was a refined daughter of Irish immigrants who disapproved of her match with James O'Neill. Eugene's parents were Irish Catholics. The father was always a stern figure of authority and mother a nurturing parent. She bore three sons in ten years of marriage but was overtaken by guilt and anguish of having lost her second son in infancy. Embittered with life as well as with Jamess touring, she chose to live life in a drug induced stupor.

Eugene O' Neill spent his childhood touring and travelling in humdrum of theatre artists and later part in distraught boarding schools. He became highly vulnerable and insecure, not only about his parents but also himself. He was twenty-six when he had tuberculosis. It was only after a touch of tuberculosis that he introspected upon his dangerous and toxic way of wanderlust living and turned to writing to find solace. His plays had an intensely personal point of view. They echoed scathing scarring effects of his family's tangled and tragic relationships.

Eugene O'Neill's father and elder brother died of alcoholism and his beloved mother gave into morphine addiction. He married thrice and became father of three children of whom one son committed suicide and other drifted into a life of emotional instability. He cut off his ties with the daughter as she married Charlie Chaplain who was twice her age. All this brought about a dichotomy in Eugene's thoughts that led to his strongly intimate and dramatic style of writing.

Eugene O'Neill was exceedingly influenced by Swedish dramatist August Strindberg and publicly acknowledged his debt to him. He also owed his writing style to Russian dramatist Anton Chekhov and Norwegian dramatist Henrik Ibsen. His sparkling and piercing dramas emanated from life's challenges. Eugene O'Neill found himself among the radical thinkers like John Reed and anarchists like Terry Carlin. Accompanied by Terry Carlin, his Irish mentor, he reached Provincetown where he found congenial companions among the radicals. Subsequently, Provincetown owners staged several of Eugene O'Neill's short plays. In 1920, Eugene O'Neill's reputation as the leading dramatist of America became established and he became sure of himself.

Writing during the roaring twenties Eugene O'Neill's works had not only realism and social protest but also a strong, cynical, and sarcastic undercurrents of materialism wherein intrinsic emotions which were rooted in spiritual fundamentalism were dramatized. Entombing the human soul in the grits of insatiability, he scrutinized the profound concealed skirmishes that kept battling in the interior recesses of human mind. He represented American intellectuals who abhorred the commercialization of civilization.

Eugene O'Neill, therefore, single handily made drama a socio-cultural medium to showcase the human side of a celebrated artist. He also explored the dilemma of the modern man in deciphering the truth behind their existence, dreams, and identity. American drama bloomed under the tutelage of Eugene O'Neill thereby making his place permanent in the galaxy of timeless and classic writers. His literary outputs affirm the multi-dimensional perspectives voiced with determination by the writer, Oscar Cargill, who is an author and editor whose works majorly deal with the works of nineteenth and twentieth century American authors. According to him the salient features of Eugene O' Neill's works touches frightening depths of human life stepping on private, social and philosophical toes (45).

When Eugene O'Neill composed *Dynamo*, he expressed his views through a letter written to George Nathan, an esteemed American drama critic. He articulated his objective by highlighting that a playwright must talk about the real-life problems as people have little hope since science and materialism is not the solution to his problems (Clark 165). Eugene O'Neill was profoundly devoted to playwriting and wrote more than fifty plays. This prolific output made him the third most translated playwright after William Shakespeare and George Bernard Shaw. He took drama as an aesthetic and intellectual form. Not only did he use American vernacular but also focused on marginalized characters. He rejected melodrama and overblown rhetoric and centred his dramas on realism where the characters' ebb and flowed in guilt, wrath, misery, pity, forgiveness, hatred, love and passion. Unspeakable rage exploded and imploded inside his characters that were in a constant state of flux. His titillating style of articulating the ordinary in an extraordinary manner made him reach the same heights as William Shakespeare. Eugene O'Neill is the only American dramatist to have won the coveted Nobel Prize and multiple Pulitzer awards. "George Bernard Shaw called him a

'Yankee Shakespeare peopling his isle with Calibans' "(qtd. by Churchbell 1).

Nietzsche, Strindberg and Ibsen were already Eugene O'Neill's intellectual mainstays. The dramatist Eugene O'Neill conceded that he was also inspired by Carl Jung as mentioned by Eugene O'Neill's biographer, Louis Sheaffer. In the book *O' Neill: Son and Playwright,* it is mentioned that he was extremely influenced by the book *Thus Spoke Zarathustra* by Friedrich Nietzsche (Sheaffer 18). He looked around him and picked up his materials. American drama had dealt with superficial theatricality which was stifling of any creative stimulus. Eugene O'Neill burst upon the world of drama with fights, drunkenness and violent language with an emphatically American accent. He captured the psychological and emotional roots of real people in his plays.

Greek elements in Eugene O'Neill's plays are conscious borrowings. He did aim at an approximation of the Greek sense of fate in modern terms. Eugene O'Neill's conscious use of Greek myths in the plot structures of two of his finest tragedies *Desire Under the Elms* and *Mourning Becomes Electra,* are proofs of the fact that he was indebted to Greek tragedy which inspired him to utilize symbols and myths from the modern perspective. He has also performed the superb act of dispensing with the supernaturalism of Greek tragedy by replacing it with determinism to render the behavioural pattern acceptable. The resultant effect is to make the play resonate with rationalistic as well as logical temper of the age. The aim is also to administer justice according to the deeds of the character.

The autobiographical elements grew in the plays written by him. He chose for his plays' themes like social injustice and conflict of races. As Joseph Wood Krutch, an American naturalist, conservationist, writer, and critic has pointed out as a part of introduction to Eugene O'Neill's book *Nine Plays by Eugene O'Neill,* "O' Neill's life has been the story of his innumerable plays, all written with passionate and absorbing faith in the importance of the task the author has set for himself" (13).

Capital, labour as well as problem including man versus machine also attracted Eugene O'Neill's attention. He was engrossed with the theme of destiny in a society that suffered from spiritual sterility which was beautifully captured in *The Great God Brown* and *The Hairy Ape*. Eugene O' Neill endeavours to recommend cures for chaotic and directionless human beings. The resolution in *The Great God Brown* lies in the amalgamation of fragmented personalities.

Eugene O'Neill's creativity declined after 1936 when the themes related to depression and its attendant ideologies made an onrush in the theatre. Consequently, no strong impulse struck his vision as commercialism had deadened all invention. *The Iceman Cometh* appeared as a realistic study of the fragility of illusions. Years later he wrote another play that was a portrait of a tormented and self-destructive family. However, he was faced by serious illness as he was diagnosed with Parkinson's disease and it culminated in his death in 1953. He was the first American playwright to win a solid international reputation. Eugene O'Neill can never be outdated as his concerns dealt with almost all techniques of modern drama. He dealt with tragedy which is outside time. He will always be reminisced for his invaluable contribution to the field of drama.

John Gassner, a noted theatre critic, writer, and editor, a respected anthologist, and an esteemed professor of drama, sums up Eugene O'Neill's contributions to drama by declaring that if faults are found in Eugene O'Neill's work than the entire American stage is faulty, if there are merits those are worth striving and straining towards significant drama (qtd. in Mundra 1). Steven F. Bloom, President of the Eugene O'Neill Society and acelebrated professor and renowned critic of Eugene O'Neill, emphasizes that in the early twentieth century Eugene O'Neill created the stage for serious American drama, which grew and flourished into the twenty first century (Bloom 61).

GIRISH KARNAD: BIOGRAPHY AND WRITING STYLE

Apart from studying Eugene O'Neill the study also includes works of India's celebrated and prolific dramatist Girish Karnad. He was born on 19 May, 1938 in Matheran, Maharashtra and raised in Karnataka. Born to an affluent and successful medical practitioner, he came across strolling groups of players in post-independent India called as the *Natak* companies or *Mandali's*. These *Natak* companies toured countryside. In Introduction to *"Three Plays"* Girish Karnad himself admits to spending post-harvest nights watching the traditional *Yashagana* performances.

Girish Karnad completed his graduation from Karnataka and moved to Mumbai, Maharashtra wherein he saw theatre, which was at its full glory. He watched August Strindberg's *Miss Julie*, who was a famous Swedish playwright, novelist and short-story writer and a stalwart of Expressionist drama. The play influenced Girish Karnad to understand the powerful journey drama made him travel. He admits that the walk through drama was emotionally and physically draining which was an agonising ceremony of introducing Girish Karnad to world drama. The play was surprisingly scandalous and emotionally draining since Girish Karnad grew up in traditional family where the notion of candidly laying bare the carnal desires was considered shockingly profane.

However, it left an ineffaceable smear on his mind and stirred his ethics and integrity. It was this journey from Karnataka's *Natak Mandali's* to Mumbai's mesmerizing theatre that made Girish Karnad take up playwriting earnestly. Henrik Ibsen's naturalistic drama also inspired Girish Karnad and through him he was swayed by G.B. Shaw's plays. William Shakespeare inspired him substantially. But Kannada drama left a profound and unfathomable impact on him. He had a profound interest in Kannada drama and therefore represented its best traits in his works.

Girish Karnad and his contemporaries had to choose between literary traditions of the west and east. They were also left to choose techniques, styles and themes which were to form the core of Indian literary scene post-independence. Girish Karnad acknowledged this fact in the Author's Introduction to *"Three Plays"* he said that the writers of newly independent India found themselves caught between a tension of following the west or their own cultural traditions, tension to choose between cultural past and its colonial history and lastly the tension to follow various visionary paths. He said he chose to centre his plays in history (1). R.K. Dhawan, Indian writer, editor and critic scrutinizes Girish Karnad's influences and asserts that Girish Karnad was equally influenced by both category of playwrights from India and the west. This allowed him to gain a bigger bandwidth and themes to work with (10).

Girish Karnad came from a close-knit family. He was the first one to go abroad for higher studies. This burdened him to the extent of expressing his inner turmoil through writing a play and that too in the language of his childhood, Kannada. Born to Konkani, fostered in Kannada, instructed in English and refined in Marathi and Hindi, Girish Karnad handled all of them with ease but preferred to do this creative writing in Kannada. Kannada was his language of choice by way of which he showcased the present with the kaleidoscope of the past. Kirtinath Kurtkoti's history of Kannada literature made him conclude that Indians writers as compared to celebrated writers of other countries did not handle Indian history as adroitly as the others like Shakespeare or Brecht.

Kirtinath Kurtkoti in his Introduction to *Hayavadana* praised Girish Karnad for providing a congenial environment for the growth of Kannada drama, he remarked that, "Girish Karnad has brought to drama the first- hand knowledge of the practical demands of the stage and a better understanding of dramatic style and technique" (69). Girish Karnad's literary exercise had contacts with the living age and stage. He sought to find and define *"Indianness"* in drama and brought to light the drama that embodied traditions of India. His plays although drew heavily from the rich sources of myths and folklore, however they were thoroughly modern in spirit and outlook. They concealed a rare sophistication and sensibility that resonated in his drama. His plays dealt with the modern man whose gradual erosion of ethics and moralities were unabashedly portrayed in his plays.

Girish Karnad's plays grappled with dualism in an individual's personality. The first one is the social facade that is worn for the world to see and second is the personal psyche which is the real one. The characters yearned for perfection and completeness in the complex world of twisted relations. King Yayati wanted eternal youth and asked his son to sacrifice his youth so as to enjoy a life of unbridled debauchery. Padmini wanted best of the head and heart so she transposed the heads of Kapila and Devdatta to find her complete man. Rani only yearned for a lovable husband whose replacement she found in a snake.

Swinging between traditional and modern Girish Karnad echoes societal predicaments. He composed powerful and painful plays with spitfires of questions and volcanic emotional outbursts. He handled the pertinent question of identity skilfully. His plays efficiently validated the powerful capacity of Indian drama in English to invigorate itself by using native themes and conventions of Folk and *Natak* Companies. M. K. Naik, a renowned Indian scholar has rightly remarked that Indian writers of drama must go back to their roots in order to find the store house of their rich culture, history and traditions. They should delve deep into folk dramas written in Sanskrit and *Prakrits*. By doing so they can cure the 'sick man' of Indian Literature in English and bring back the artistic glory of the past into their present and celebrate the future (43-44).

Girish Karnad's dramatic contribution starts from *Yayati* and includes *Boiled Beans on Toast* which showcases Indian theatre's trajectory. When he went out of India for higher studies, amidst the intense emotional commotion, he wrote *Yayati*. It was by chance that Girish Karnad became a dramatist. He had often expressed his willingness of being a poet however, when he faced an internal turmoil he started writing a drama. It was at the age of twenty-two that he realized that he could bloom into a playwright.

Yayati reworks a *Mahabharata* myth and explores identity quest, patriarchal dominance and the subaltern concerns. Yayati, Pooru,

Chitralekha, Devayani and Sharmistha are impeccably drawn characters. These characters are in a constant state of flux as they try to manoeuvre their ways through the maze of questions dealing with filial responsibility and identity quest. Due to this these characters find themselves in ludicrous circumstances that makes them lonesome, alienated, rootless and helpless in the society.

Hayavadana is the most representative of his plays. It deals with archetypal theme, underlying mythical patterns, identifiable character-types, folk theatre conventions i.e. use of mask, curtains, dolls, story within story, use of images of *Kali, Ganesh, Rudra* etc, and allegorical connotations are some of its characteristic features as well. *Hayavadana,* is about two friends, Devadatta and Kapila, who are in love with the same girl, Padmini. Devadatta is intellectually sound and Kapila has a strong body. The existential crisis in which Padmini finds herself is the choice she has to make between the head of Devadatta who has the body of Kapila and the head of Kapila that has the body of Devadatta. This pursuit points out to the old knowledge of head being supreme.

Nagamandala showcases a story of male chauvinist Appanna who subjugates his wife. Rani is caught in a loveless marriage as Appanna locks her up and is always with his concubine. With the turn of events a shape shifting *naga* falls in love Rani and regularly visits her at night. In the play Rani's plight is agonising, challenging, realistic and existential in touch which sets her on an imprudent pursuit for her identity. The play deals with gender bias and subjugation of woman in a patriarchal Indian orthodox society.

Saryug Yadav, a writer and critic, regards Girish Karnad to be a pioneer among his contemporaries who have experimented with culture (15). Girish Karnad's experiments with drama created the path for future dramatists. P. Hari Padma Rani, critic and writer is also vocal about Girish Karnad's contribution to the drama in India by creating a blend of not only his own techniques but borrowing them from folk theatre and classical drama (18).

BRIEF SUMMARY OF THE SELECTED PLAYS

This book proposes pertinent questions on the characters created by Girish Karnad and Eugene O'Neill and their pursuit of identity. They also consider subaltern issues and the ways myths play a prominent role. *The Hairy Ape, Desire Under Elms* and *The Great God Brown* are the selected plays from American playwright's Eugene O'Neill's dramatic oeuvre. The three selected plays from India's contemporary voice Girish Karnad are *Yayati, Hayavadana* and *Nagamandala*.

The Hairy Ape was written in 1922. It was an expressionist play that showcased the angst of a Transatlantic stoker, Yank. Yank is proud of his masculinity and his ability to propel the ship forward with his physical strength. He is the king of the stokehole as he is burly and muscular. He calls the ship his home and takes extreme pride in his work. Yank is friends with Paddy and Long. Paddy lives in the past and keeps on reminiscing about the past and his work on clipper ship. Long is a Marxist and tells Yank about the smug upper classes and an association of working-class people called as International workers of the world (I.W.W). Yank is content with his work and life. However, one day Mildred, the daughter of the owner of Nazareth steel plans to visit the stokehole in order to see how the other half lives. Mildred is comfortably placed on the promenade deck that abounds in sunlight and fresh ocean air. She along with her aunt plan to visit the stokehole. Mildred is dressed in all white and on seeing the coal dust covered stokehole and the stokers is taken aback after she comes face to face with Yank. She turns his world upside down when she calls him a hairy ape and collapses. Yank sets out on a journey to belong and find his identity in a materialistic society who considers human beings as just numbers. Ultimately, Yank finds solace in an ape's arms as he is smothered to death by the ape.

The second play of Eugene O'Neill that has been selected as a part of the study is *Desire Under Elms* which was written in 1924. This play showcases Eugene O'Neill's ability to unite modern drama with Greek. It is heavily influenced by 'myths of Oedipus', 'Medea' and 'Hippolytus'. The play revolves around the ownership of a New England farm that has sinister maternal presence of two brooding Elms on either side of the house. Ephraim Cabot has two sons from his first marriage, Peter and Simeon who leave as soon as the play starts. Eben is Ephraim's son from his second marriage. He wishes to avenge his mother's death. Ephraim Cabot is responsible for Eben's mother's death as he only believes in hard work and slogs his sons to work on the farm. Ephraim Cabot who is seventy-six years old has now married Abbie Puttenham who is thirty-five years old. Abbie is a shrewd and manipulative girl who wants to own the farm after Ephraim Cabot dies. She is also attracted to her stepson Eben. With time she has a change of heart and starts to like Eben. Eben at first doesn't like Abbie however, with the passage of time falls in love with her. They both consummate their love and Abbie becomes pregnant and gives birth to a son. Ephraim Cabot doesn't know about their affair and is very happy to know that he still can beget a son. Ephraim Cabot casually discuses with Eben the ownership of the farm which now will be with the new-born baby. Eben thinks that Abbie tricked him into getting the farm and in a fit of rage runs to sheriff to complain. Abbie in order to prove her love for Eben, kills the new born child. However, when he comes back, he shares the blame with Abbie and accepts her fate.

The third selected play is *The Great God Brown* which was written in 1926. This play is an Expressionistic play that makes use of masks to show the difference between two types of persona. One is a public face that wears the mask and other is private maskless face. William A. Billy Brown is successful architect. He is friends with Dion Anthony who is also an architect. Both of their fathers were business partners. Dion has an artistic and creative personality but as Billy Brown bullied him and made fun of his craft so Dion started wearing a Pan-like mask so as to hide his creativity. Both of them love Margaret but Margaret finds the sensitive artistic Dion more attractive and marries him. However, Margaret loves Dion only with the mask and fails to recognise him without it. So, Dion lives a dual life even with his wife. He dissipates all the money he gets from selling off his father's company and ultimately starts ghost-designing buildings at Billy Brown's office. Dion finds solace in the arms of maternal Cybel but Brown ensures that he buys out

Cybel so that Dion has no place to rest his artistic soul. By the end even Dion's mask turns from mischievous pan like to demonic Mephistophelian. Dion is unable to handle his interior tussle and outside materialistic society so dies at Billy's bourgeois like house. Billy Brown always wanted to be like Dion and aspired to live his life so he takes up Dion's mask and starts living Dion's life. He starts loving Margaret and being a good husband as well as a father. However, he is unable to handle Dion's creative mask and ultimately is charged with his own death. He is shot dead at end. Margaret continues to love Dion's mask.

Girish Karnad's first selected play is *Yayati* which was written in 1960.Girish Karnad conceived Yayati when he himself was faced with the difficulty of leaving behind his family to study abroad. The play is based on a myth from *The Mahabharata* of a king named Yayati who longed for eternal youth and wanted to exchange his old age with his young son. However, Girish Karnad turns the myth on its head. Yayati is married to great sage Shukracharya's daughter Devayani. Yayati is expecting the arrival of his newly married son Pooru and his wife Chitralekha. Meanwhile, Sharmistha , a *Rakshashi* princess, who used to be Devayani's friend but is now making her life a living hell, has a heated argument with Devayani . Yayati intervenes and tires to reason out with Sharmistha.

Sharmistha narrates to Yayati the reason behind their tortured relationship. Devayani's father is Sharmistha's father Brahmin. She and Devayani used to be thick friends but one day their blouses got exchanged and Devayani humiliated Sharmistha to the extent that she pushed Devayani into a well. Yayati rescued Devayani from the well with his right hand and as per the norms had to marry Devayani since he held her by her right hand. Sharmistha's father punishes her by making her Devayani's slave. Sharmistha tries to drink poison but is stopped by Yayati with right hand. This again brings to light the norm of getting married if held by right hand. They both consummate their marriage on Pooru and Chitralekha's nuptial bed. When Devayani gets to know about this she runs to her father who curses Yayati to old age and decrepitude but since he saved his daughter from drowning in the well he tells that

Yayati can exchange his old age with anybody's youth. Yayati is confident that his Kingdom's people will be eager to exchange but not a soul comes forward. It Is Pooru, Yayati's son who is ready to exchange his youth. Sharmistha is an eye opener for both as she turns out to be their voice of reason and discourages Pooru from doing this. Yayati however faces Chitralekha's wrath as she demands that he sleeps with her since he has taken her husband's youth. Chitralekha's commits suicide that opens Yayati's eyes and gives back youth to Pooru. Old Yayati now retires with Sharmistha and asks Pooru to rule well.

The second selected play from the dramatic oeuvre of Girish Karnad is *Hayavadana.* It was written in 1972. *Hayavadana* has been taken from Sanskrit folk tale and Thomas Mann's story of *The Transposed Heads. It* deals with the story of five fractured and broken identities namely Devadatta, Kapila, Padmini, Padmini's son and Hayavadana. Girish Karnad has taken elements from ancient traditions and used them here. The play deliberates upon whether the head is superior or the body is supreme. All the characters are in search for completeness. Hayavadana is a celestial being who seeks completeness as he has a horse's head and a human body. Bhagavata suggests him to go the famous *Kali* temple and asks her to make him complete. Devadatta is a poet and starts to like Padmini. He is friends with muscular Kapila. Padmini and Devadatta get married. However, after some time she starts liking Kapila which is visible in her actions. The three plan to go to a fair in Ujjain and on the way end up going to a Goddess *Kali* temple, which is in ruins, where Devadatta offers his head to Goddess *Kali* out of reverence for fulfilling all his wishes.

When Devadatta doesn't return Kapila searches for him and finds him beheaded in Goddess *Kali's* temple. Out of his love and friendship he also chops off his head so as to follow him in his deeds. After waiting when Padmini goes to the temple she finds both of them beheaded and out of fear of being considered a whore for whom two men laid their lives she also takes the sword to offer her head. However, she is interrupted by Goddess *Kali* who insists that since of the three she is the only one to have spoken the truth so she wishes to grant her wish and revive the men. In her excitement she mixes them up and puts Devadatta's head on Kapila's body and vice versa. Now Padmini gets what she really wanted a sharp brain and an agile body that is the best of both the men. The man with Kapila's head and Devadatta's body retires to the forest. Padmini and Devadatta now enjoy complete marital bliss. However, after a while Devadatta's head makes his body regain its former shape and now Padmini starts dreaming about Kapila which is informed by the Dolls that act as a chorus. Padmini goes to forest and finds Kapila who is now tough and muscular. Devadatta reaches Kapila's house searching for Padmini and Kapila suggests that they all live like Pandavas and Draupadi. Devadatta rejects this idea and asks him to take up a sword and fight. Both men die fighting and Padmini performs *Sati*. Padmini hands over her mute child to Bhagavata who after seeing Hayavadana starts laughing.

Nagamandala is the third selected play from Girish Karnad's works. The plot has been taken from Kannada folktales. The flames, story and man are like the chorus that inform about the major happenings of the play. The play highlights the plight of a newly married Rani who is caught in a loveless marriage. Her husband Appanna goes to a concubine and comes home only for lunch. He keeps Rani locked in the house. Appanna's mother's friend handicap Kurudavva visits Rani and gives her two magical roots so as to make Appanna fall in love with her. However, when Rani makes a paste and mixes it, it turns red and she pours it onto an ant-hill where a shape shifting *Naga* lives who gets instantly smitten by her. The *naga* now impersonates as her husband and visits her at nights. They both find each other's company fulfilling and ultimately consummate their marriage. Rani announces her pregnancy to Appanna who gets angry and calls her a whore for he knows he hasn't slept with her. He goes to the village council who ask Rani to take the chastity test of either holding a red-hot iron in hand or plunging the hand in boiling oil and lastly to swear by holding a cobra in one's hand. Rani accepts to take the Cobra/*Naga* test.

When Rani takes the test, the shape shifting *Naga* coils around hand and moves over her shoulders like a garland. The villagers consider her as a goddess incarnate and so now Appanna is made to spend his life in Rani's service. So, Rani gets whatever she wished for, a devoted husband and a happy married life. The play is known for having multiple ending as in one Rani lives a happy and content life. The other ending shows the *Naga* sliding up her shoulders and resting in Rani's long tresses and lastly Appanna kills the *Naga* and Rani ensures that their son performs his last rites and *Naga* is remembered every year as rituals are performed by their son to commemorate *Naga's* death.

The transcendental quality of playwrights works makes contemporary lurk through the veils of antiquity. The heroes are contemporary and agonize for their socio-economic status. On one hand Eugene O'Neill reintroduces the grandeur of Greek tragedy and transmutes the Greek myths into modern insights and on the other, Girish Karnad gives the traditional mask a contemporary twist. Both take modern characters and weave them into current philosophical ideas to yield a new connotation for the new generation of readers.

The research seeks to understand and appreciate Eugene O' Neill and Girish Karnad as the forerunners of Modern drama in America and India respectively and strives to focus on the usage of myth by both playwrights and interpretation of it from present times. The textual scrutiny will examine the issues of identity as taken up by both the playwrights, therefore, explore the plight of subalterns as depicted in their works

The book is organized in three chapters preceded by "Introduction" and followed by "Conclusion". The "Introduction" provides the general rationale and approach to the thesis; briefly introduces drama and its European and Indian history. The introduction also takes selected biographical information about Eugene O' Neill and Girish Karnad to justify the choice of Eugene O'Neill and Girish Karnad as the main focus of this study. The aims and objectives of the study, methodology, and techniques that are used to present the study are also mentioned. It also considers a wide array of literature review undertaken to understand the research that has already been done by umpteen scholars and writers. Chapter two to five are written using textual analysis as the tool of research along with literary criticism as its method of analysis of six selected plays.

Chapter one takes into consideration myths and their reworking by both the playwrights as it uses mythical perspective as its methodology. This chapter compels one to undertake a re-assessment and re-evaluation of myths and probes into their modern adaptation. The second chapter probes deeper into the quest of identity by taking a cultural perspective on Identity crisis. This methodology helps to appreciate the works and to read by analysing the selected plays. The third chapter deals with subaltern concerns and critically looks at gender and various subaltern issues. Feminist and class concerns are also highlighted in this chapter. "Conclusion" offers a quick recapitulation of the foregoing discussion, discusses the level of convergence and divergence of both the playwrights and presents the conclusion. It also tries to identify areas for further study and research.

The methodological approach used here is critical in nature. The qualitative method of analysis will be used along with a textual approach that will map the contribution of Eugene O'Neill and Girish Karnad. The content analysis will be done pertaining to their relevance in the present scenario as well as their contributions to the immense world of literature with a special focus on myths, identity crisis and subaltern issues. The appropriate methodology is designed to serve this purpose.

I

CONFIGURATION OF MYTH: EUGENE O'NEILL AND GIRISH KARNAD

Mythopoeia is a Hellenistic term which means 'myth making'; a narrative genre in modern literature where a myth is recreated by the author. The word was made popular by JRR Tolkien in the 1930s who created *The Hobbit*. The authors of this genre amalgamate traditional mythological themes and archetypes into fiction. Mythopoeia is also the act of making (creating) such mythologies. Notable mythopoeic authors include

C. S. Lewis, Robert W. Chambers, H.P. Lovecraft, George MacDonald, and Lord Dunsany. While many literary works integrate mythic themes, only a few approaches the dense self- referential and purpose of mythopoeia. It has been discovered that mythology, rather than arising out of centuries of oral tradition, has been penned over a short period of time by a single author or small group of collaborators.

As opposed to fantasy world or fictional universe aimed at the evocation of detailed world with well-ordered histories, geographies, and laws of nature, mythopoeia aims at imitating and including real-world mythology, specifically created to bring mythology to modern readers (Mythopoeia 1). It consists of a story-telling that involves an extensive, deep, rich mythology the author has constructed over many years. It is existential and profound, played out via characters in story, yet driven by a greater plan. The myths used in narration are primarily aiming at transposing the world of people, events, struggle, and the nature of this world onto the mythic landscape of the human mind and heart. The literary works under this genre involve exploring the vast architecture of the self; where Gods, worlds, and tragedy collide, huge landscapes and legions of characters engage in a conflict and struggle that wages fiercely in the author's unconscious mind (Stokely 25).

Myths have fascinated human mind from time immemorial as a central issue in his/her efforts to define meaning of religion, culture and history by providing new life to art and literature, and have remained as the motivating force behind the artistic explorations. The word "myth" comes from the Greek word 'mythos' which means an ancient traditional story of gods or heroes (Myth). According to Leon L. Bram and Robert Phillips, myth is "…a tale of obscure or forgotten origin, fundamentally religious in characters having a supernatural frame of reference and serving to explain or sanctify some concept, usage, institution or natural phenomenon (95). The Greeks were the first ones to study myths thoroughly and that's why they were called, "…allegories which veil deep moral meanings" (95).

In common parlance, a myth is a story that deals with Gods, supernatural beings and heroes. It is traditional which means that it was transmitted orally for many ages. It is extremely challenging to arrive at any single definition of myth. For example, myths can be stories about ancient events that define and sustain notions of community. However, a myth can also be a fabrication or act of false speech that is, nevertheless, ideologically persuasive. It is a legendary or a traditional story which is usually androcentric which may not be supported by facts or real explanations.

They primarily concentrate on demigods or deities, and describe rites, practices, and natural phenomenon and the hero who will have divine qualities but will always have a status inferior to Gods but will have qualities that will put them at a higher pedestal from the sapiens. Characteristically, a myth involves historical and gothic elements. M.H. Abrams in his *A Glossary of Literary Terms* defines myths as, "In classical Greek, mythos signifies any story or plot, whether true or invented…In its central modern significance, however, a myth is one story in a mythology —a system of hereditary stories which were once believed to be true by a particular cultural group" (170). Abrams lays emphasizes on culture and the ability of myths to transcend time and be applicable universally.

There are many types of myths, such as classic myths, religious myths, and modern myths. Classical myths are inspired by the Greek and Roman myths and are a product of how they are received by the different cultures. They are generally made popular by the oral traditions. Religious myths under this approach are traditional such as the biblical ones which are read symbolically rather than literally. Myths are an important element of religion and consist of concepts, which are important to understand and interpret certain concepts. People all around the world try to rework or embroider the existing ones to create modern myths. They originated as artistic creation, although their creators may have drawn from earlier myths. Modern mythical superheroes like Superman will have the good qualities of mythical heroes along with supernatural powers (Encyclopaedia). They are predominantly ancient, and happen to have ruled the world when science, philosophy, and technology were not very precise; it was myths that explained natural phenomena, and described rituals and ceremonies to the people.

There is a difference in myth and mythology which is explained by the renowned Indian dramatist, Girish Karnad in his Prologue to *Yayati*. He said, "Our play this evening deals with an ancient myth. But, let me rush to explain, it is not 'mythological'. Heaven forbids! A mythological aim to plunge us into the sentiment of devotion" (Karnad; YAYA 14). According to Northrop Frye, "a mythology rooted in a specific society transmits a heritage of shared allusion and verbal experience in time, and so mythology helps to create a cultural history…a unified mythology is a powerful instrument of social authority and coercion (51). The ability of myths to form a collective opinion is also highlighted by Vico, he says "only from mythology can we discover the religion, morals, law, and social life of early society (435). He further adds that myths are neither false nor allegories but reflect the collective outlook of an age.

Another point, that is worth noting, is the difference in myth, legends and folktales. A myth becomes a legend if the hero is a normal human being and not a supernatural being. A folktale is a myth that is not a part of systematic mythology. Myths are usually regarded as fairy tales or beautifully narrated flights of imagination invented by primitive people for their amusement or consolation in the face of baffling natural phenomena.

Drawing a contrast between Indian myth and Greek myth, Surbhi Sharma has described Indian myths "as classical myths as well as religious". She draws "similarities between the Indian Gods and the Hellenistic Gods like Indra and Zeus", furthermore, "the concept of Holy Trinity is found in the Greek myths as Zeus, Hades and Poseidon, in Bible it is the Father, the Son and the Holy Ghost and in Hinduism it is Brahma, Vishnu and Mahesh" (21).

The debate about the difference and similarity in mythologies has been never ending. Sister Nivedita vividly explains the difference amongst mythology, culture and common life, primarily her fascination for the Indian mythologies and their influence on common life:

The stories of India, the Ramayana, the Mahabharata the legends of Krishna, Buddha and Shiva and others from Puranas and Vedas are among the most beautiful in the world, while the characters and ideals they represent are some of the loftiest, most noble and the most enchanting the world has ever seen. To Indians however, the characters in these myths are not just superhuman beings of some hoary past rather, they are paradigms. This is why these religions and myths are still living today. Even now Rama, Krishna, Arjuna, Yudhishthira, Vasishtha, Vidura, Sita, Savitri, Nala, Lakshmana, Bharata, Hanuman and Buddha serve as paradigms for their ideal ruler, hero, householder, hermit, devotee, wife, husband, brother, servant, monk and so on. (144)

Mythopoeic is something in which man still persists to find meaning and content of his experience. The myths afford the artist both the necessary artistic control to explore his subject and means of generalization. Though differing at points, these myths contribute to a unified vision, testify the facts and experience of life, and serve as viable framework dramatizing modern dilemmas and conflicts implicit in contemporary situations. Writers have used myths and symbols evolved through human experience. Like the western dramatists e.g., Luigi Pirandello, Jean Giraudoux, Jean Anouilh and Jean Paul Sartre among others, modern American dramatists led by Eugene O' Neill sought to appease their dramatic quests with the perennial meanings as found in myths and symbols and interwove them extensively in the themes of their drama.

In the comparative study of Eugene O'Neill and Girish Karnad, the configuration of myth plays a pivotal role, serving as a rich tapestry that weaves together cultural, historical, and symbolic elements. Both playwrights skilfully incorporate mythic narratives into their works, tapping into the collective unconscious and deep-seated cultural motifs to explore the complexities of human experiences and societal dynamics. By drawing upon these mythic elements, O'Neill and Karnad bring forth a wealth of symbolism, archetypes, and cultural resonances that add layers of depth and meaning to their plays.

For O'Neill, the influence of Greek tragedies is evident in works such as *Mourning Becomes Electra*. Here, he configures myth by intertwining mythological archetypes and motifs, exploring themes of fate, guilt, and familial relationships. The use of Greek myths allows O'Neill to tap into universal narratives and archetypal patterns, creating a sense of timelessness and inherent human struggles within his characters. By configuring myth in this way, O'Neill expands the scope of his works and invites audiences to engage with broader existential questions.

Similarly, Karnad draws upon historical and mythological narratives from Indian folklore, effectively configuring myth to blend the personal and political dimensions of identity. In plays like Tughlaq, Karnad incorporates mythical elements to explore the complexities of power dynamics, the quest for legitimacy, and the tensions between personal desires and political responsibilities. By configuring myth within the context of Indian history, Karnad not only provides a rich cultural backdrop but also challenges prevailing narratives and offers alternative perspectives on identity and power.

In examining the configuration of myth in O'Neill and Karnad's works, this research aims to analyze the impact of these mythic elements on the construction and portrayal of characters' identities. Both playwrights utilize myth to delve into the nuances of individual and collective identities, exploring the ways in which cultural, historical, and mythical dimensions shape and influence the characters' sense of self. The configuration of myth allows O'Neill and Karnad to delve into the complexities of human identity, probing questions of self-discovery, cultural inheritance, and the negotiation of societal expectations.

Furthermore, the incorporation of myth in the plays of O'Neill and Karnad also gives voice to the subaltern, the marginalized and oppressed groups in society. By configuring myth to include the experiences and perspectives of the subaltern, the playwrights challenge dominant narratives and provide a platform for the expression and exploration of marginalized voices. Through the use of mythic narratives, O'Neill and Karnad highlight the agency and struggles of subaltern characters, shedding light on their resilience, resistance, and aspirations within their respective social contexts.

By examining the configuration of myth in the works of Eugene O'Neill and Girish Karnad, this book seeks to unravel the intricate interplay between myth, identity, and subalternity. It aims to shed light on how these playwrights utilize mythic elements to explore the complexities of human existence, challenge dominant narratives, and give voice to the marginalized. Through this exploration, a deeper understanding of the transformative power of theatre emerges, showcasing its ability to engage with mythic dimensions and evoke profound insights into the human condition.

EUGENE O'NEILL: USAGE OF MYTHS

Eugene O' Neill the paterfamilias of modern American drama has generated a lot of interest. He was a progenitor of Avant-garde modern drama in America. He endowed his works with a new urgency and seriousness almost equal to the European dramatists of the early twentieth century he gave a new impetus to the American drama enlarging its scope for its thematic content and theatrical innovations. Before him the American stage was awash with genteel, sentimental comedies of inane merit based on standardized, flamboyant and familiar themes. He pioneered the drama of serious realism with uncompromising honesty.

Eugene O' Neill's plays were cardio grams of the impatient heart in which he charred the thwarted dreams and elusive hopes of his characters, the defeated lives and tormented lives whom fate rendered unrealized. He opened up the American stage to a range of lives and occupation outside the familiar middle class quotidian experience. He dislodged the contemporary American dramatic practices with rigor; rebelling against the shibboleths and provided new substance to his audacious experiments exposing drama to new vistas of freedom with his use of natural symbols, chorus, crowds and their choreographic movements, asides, masks and interior monologue to name a few. He was offered bouquets of critical encomiums and accolades as well as lashed with vituperative tirades. There is an emotional honesty and sincerity of effort in his works. Through his use of over brimming compassion, sweep of sympathy and richness and intensity of the themes he achieves an unconventional style of using myths in his drama.

However, the use of myths, archetypal patterns, and symbols in O'Neill's plays have not been given an unbiased, balanced and comprehensive assessment, though there have been a few fragmented attempts to study myths in his works. The entire corpus of his plays has not been subject to such a magnified treatment. His plays echo with mythical patterns and allusions, for he saw in myths an indispensable means of conveying deeper meaning. He imbued his plays with myths. Like the romantics he used archetypal symbols, ritual patterns of myths to express the elemental appetites, passions and such forces that affect man's behaviour in a given circumstance. He used myths to describe basic urges and inexplicable forces at work in a particular social milieu. The myths operate at various experimental levels in the plays even though there is no conscious effort made by O'Neill to provide myths to show their specific roles in the interpretation of subterranean human cravings.

Eugene O'Neill created his own myths from the attitudes of contemporary American society as reflected in his plays in the archetypal forms such as the myth of American Dream, of Innocence and the Fall, the myth of Eden or the Quest. Thomas E. Porter examined the American plays to discern structures and patterns created by fixed cultural attitudes, recurrent images as those of suburbia or small town, or stereotypes like salesman (Porter 11). Culture is primarily changing and continuous process, accommodates with itself the changing realities of life through the dialectics of thesis, antitheses and synthesis. Thus, myth becomes a sort of a permanent foil, a predicament and pervading idealization of life against the current realities of an advancing culture.

The myth of Eden that considers America as a paradise is one of such cultural beliefs and attitudes. O'Neill used it in his play by adopting it negatively because of the conflict between the weariness of actual life and the ideal of paradise. He interpreted the contemporary experience in terms of waste land, corruption and degeneration. Contrary to the writers' exalted tone about American life and values as inherited of Eden, he viewed that the innocent American Adam and his ideal milieu were figments of imagination. David Madden, an American novelist and critic postulates that there are two major American Dream myths- "the Old Testament idea of a Paradise hopelessly lost; followed by endless nightmare sufferings and New Testament's idea of a Paradise that a new American Adam will eventually regain". He further explains that the "most serious fiction is slanted against the New Testament vision, hope for clear vision lies in the ambiguous area between Paradise Lost and Paradise Regained" (Madden XXIX).

The myth of American dream emerged out of American myth of paradise. The myth of Eden becomes a theological metaphor of man's relation to God. Its significant meaning concerns moral, cultural and psychological life of America. The Arcadia theme originated out of it in the traditional belief that nature is a continuous source of pleasure and bounty, and a symbol of perfect life (Miller 194). A myth assimilates and crystallizes tradition and cultural experiences of a society into a permanent system of values in a higher imaginative form. In this way, it becomes a cultural product generally, as Wilder puts it, "dreaming soul of the race telling its story" (Haberman 117).

MYTHS IN THE HAIRY APE

Eugene O'Neill has wed tied various mythical and symbolic elements to texture of his play, *The Hairy Ape*. The various mythical elements, symbolism and the expressionistic techniques help in formation of a new myth. An insight may help to bring out the association between these mythical patterns, symbols, culture, and the meaning that the playwright created and celebrated.

Myth is an uncritically accepted story that provides a model to interpret current experience. Joseph Campbell an American Professor of Literature who worked on American comparative mythology and religion, suggested a sterling point in the quest for mythic coherence, he said that "classical monomyth deals with human maturation and integration in which the hero departs from his home in search of adventures, slays a dragon, and then returns" (30). To him, the paradigm for thousands of primitive and classical folk tales, fairy tales and religious myths is based upon rites of initiation. The plot-structure of the classical monomyth can be schematized as such: (i) The Hero departs (grows up in the face of external dangers and threats); (ii) encounters with fabulous Jaegers, and he emerges victorious; (iii) the Hero returns and accepts social or familial responsibility or accepts community leadership. By raising a family, he accomplishes the responsibilities of the next generation (30-31).

Eugene O' Neill uses the divergent form of the American monomyth because this kind of mythic consciousness is not explicit in his plays. There were various reasons for the change. The American culture did not have a mythology. The people also decried the Bible, which served as its alternative. The loss of mythic and communal ideals also prompted want of heroism in American culture. Further, the scepticism and refusal to idealize, and lack of shared values inspiring to a common effort of an idealized hero were also instrumental in changing the concept of the Hero.

In *The Hairy Ape,* the American paradise is infested with the evils of capitalism depriving it of its Eden like innocence and potency. The myth of democracy is punctured by inequality, exploitation and spiritual exhaustion. The characters are haunted by the miasma of past. They say: "We ain't. We weren't born this rotten way. All men are born free and ekal. That's in the bleedin' Bible, maties. But what d'they care for the Bible- them lazy, bloated swine what travels first cabin?" (Batra; THA 84).

Yank arrives on the scene. He expresses his angst against the prevailing social order which exploits the very working class on which it grows and feeds on. He becomes a sworn enemy of the capitalistic class and seeks gratification in eulogizing his strength. He says about the capitalists, "Dey're just baggage," and "I'm at de bottom, -I'm de end! I'm de start!.. I'm de ting in coal day makes it goin,' I'm steam and oil for de engines: ....

I'm de ting in gold dat make it money!" (Batra; THA 86).

The community of sailors is incapable for facing these forces. They are helpless even to make their dreams materialize, and equally helpless to forget the past. Yank is resolved to fight against these forces and redeem his community from injustice, inequality and exploitation. His arrival stimulates his fellows. He tries 'to ink' how to combat with these forces. He gets furious at Mildred's sight who represents the capitalistic class. He visits Industrial Workers of the World (I.W.W.), to seek its help in overthrowing capitalistic regime. His encounter with Mildred has deprived him of his identity. His search ultimately takes him to a zoo where he is smothered by a gorilla as he tries to communicate with him.

On the surface, there is no victory for Yank, the hero, but he emerges victorious in his death because there is hope in hopelessness. He dies hoping for a better social order. His death signifies a typical achievement of "Regeneration through Violence" that is a type of American national mythology stretching back to the origins of American literature (Slotkin 19). Although Eugene O' Neill celebrated the contemporary cultural beliefs and myths of success but he also exposed their shallowness and futility in his works. He had already dismissed the myth of American Dream in an interview to Croswsel Bowen who is an American political reporter and journalist. Eugene O'Neill's Yank sneers at the myths of success, paradise and democracy, when Americans were flaunting these myths before the whole world. The playwright revealed it through the play's theme of primitiveness of the proletariat, its problems of belonging and alienation in the highly mechanized and industrialized society. Yank has lost faith in the socialist dogma or in the Bible's sanctity. In him atheism is wedded to revolutionary propaganda.

Yank, though has human attributes, is a complex symbol. He is an individual on a quest - not an individual on personal quest but a reflection of Everyman's search for belonging who is out of harmony with himself. His sufferings symbolize the sufferings of many contemporary Americans who possessed alienated souls. Since his predicament is suggestive of every modern man in general and appeals beyond time and place, his tragedy becomes the tragedy of every man.

Yank, the hairy ape, has little brain but a lot of muscles, He behaves as an ape. Again, he symbolizes the lowest man caged in a steeled society. He goes on a violent murderous spree wherein he tries to provoke people who are coming out of the church. He tries to pluck the street kerbing and to pull off a lamp post to use it as club. He punches his fist into a fat man's face who is rushing to catch a bus. His senseless behaviour takes him to prison where he becomes a sort of modem hairy ape. It is symbolic of his retrogression in a so-called progressive world. He retraces to man's early stages of evolution till he seeks brotherhood with the gorilla in the cage. He symbolizes the animalistic nature of man, the impulses and instincts which man has inherited from his biological ancestor, the ape. He symbolizes the class of stokers. He is a proletariat, a symbol of an epitomized protest against the structure of modern society against a civilization feeding on exploitation of men and his body-against modern mechanized society.

Yank, Paddy and Long symbolize present, past and future. They represent the composite altitude of the dramatist, Yank's attitude is of seeking identification with the ship, its power and factory whistles, which is shattered when he apprehends that he is controlled not by the ship but by those who own steel. The second attitude is that of Paddy whose nostalgia is wrapped in the husk' of past and he craves to return to those days of freedom and oneness which Yank resents. This attitude is pitched against Long's social anarchist longings for better future. Long represents the playwright's radical outlook who thinks that the society's structure is rotten due to the banalities of capitalistic system yet he suggests fighting with legal means, as he says, "Take it easy, comrade!

Keep your temper in check. Remember force defeats itself. It isn't our weapon. We must pursue. We must impress our demands through peaceful means- the votes of the on- marching proletarians of the bloody world!" (Batra; THA 130).

The ship symbolises modern society where the workers represent different races with their nostalgic longings. It is a microcosm of mechanized society where the pressures of existence have bent the backs of the inhabitants and given them stooping postures. Yank tries to seek belongingness with the ship but it failed him. His alienation started from the ship which could not reciprocate the faith he had put. Mildred symbolizes the rich capitalist class lacking in originality and vigour of life, but living in luxury and artificiality on the sweat of the hairy apes. Her encounter with Yank symbolizes the modern class conflict. Yank's subsequent loss of faith, joy in work and frustration suggests the state of modern industrial worker who is caged by the very steel which he produces. The Industrial Workers of the World (I.W.W.) stands for tyranny, oppression and suspicion of workers' union which in spite of providing security and fighting for the workers, suspects Yank as an agent provocateur (spy) and throw him out of their office. The Industrial Workers of the World (I.W.W.) proves to be an agent of Yank's tragedy by aggravating his frustration and alienation.

The setting and language are also symbolic. The recurrence of the word 'belong' by Yank suggests his obsession, use of clipped and uneven phrases throughout the play conveys his agitation at his alienation. The dramatist used the gorilla's growls and roars to approximate the conversation between a human being and an animal. Yank's quest for belonging from non-belonging is symbolic of the playwright's quest on religious, social, physical and familial levels. He was not able to belong anywhere. Wherever he went, he loved that place only to realize that he did not belong there ultimately. He used symbols, weird fantasy and expressionistic techniques in evoking the feeling of pressurized existence of man and the origin of human society. The play symbolizes human wishes and aspirations, which can be cherished by everybody, be it black or white, rich or poor but the dark forces of the prejudice, jealousy and misunderstanding generally nip their quest. With expressionistic devices, the playwright interprets the wider ethnic concerns of the age which still plague the mankind.

MYTHS IN DESIRE UNDER ELMS

Desire Under the Elms is an enactment of Greek and Biblical myths. Eugene O'Neill utilizes psychological and philosophical perception of myth and symbols to explore a new criterion to dramatize the effects of repression on life, and the playwright becomes a physician of souls. The psychological forces and historical milieu in which the play was conceived make the study of mythic patterns interesting. The play is replete with classical and Biblical myths. The traces of oedipal incest are explicit in the relationship between the Eben and Abbie, and again in Eben seeking out Min, a prostitute with whom his father and brothers have had sexual relationship, Edwin Engel observed, "If O'Neill has a kinship with Oedipus, it is with the complex rather than the Rex" (Engel 132). The criticism implied is only partially true. It creates a modern myth with new relationship suggesting a new interpretation of the tragedy (Carpenter 106).

The Phaedra Hippolytus myth is more consciously planted in the play which had previously been used by Euripides in *Hippolytus* and the Racine in *Phaedra*. The basic theme of these plays is the same that is the uncertain nature of man's relation to the power of terrifying forces not only beyond his control but beyond the reach of his under- standing. But Eugene O'Neill's use of the mythic properties is more in modernistic vein where Dionysius passions are still dominating, while the sources of passion and love remain mysterious.

Eugene O'Neill diverged from the original mythic source. In the Greek myth Theseus has returned with young wife Phaedra, who is immediately fascinated by her step-son Hippolytus. In this play Ephraim Cabot has brought a young wife Abbie who is attracted by Eben but Eben is not as chaste as Hippolytus who repulsed his mother's advances. Although in the beginning Eben hates Abbie for "Hate ye fur stealin' her place--here in her hum--settin' in her parlorwhar she was laid..." yet Abbie responds to Abbie's advances and she is more successful in her plans than Phaedra. She is not subjected to any kind of remorse which Phaedra underwent. In the beginning Abbie hides her passionate desire for Eben under the mask of hatred. She even poisons ears of infatuated Ephraim, "So that's the thanks I git fur marryin' ye--t' have ye change kind to Eben who hates ye, an' talk o' turnin' me out in the road," (Batra; DUE 128) Phaedra got Hippolytus exiled, so does Abbie threaten, "I'll say ye're lyin' a-purpose--an' he'll drive ye off the place!" (Batra; DUE116). Abbie's desire for Eben is for the same motive in addition to her greed for possession of farm and future security.

It is with Abbie's new baby that myth of Medea enters the theme that is the wife killing her child in order to avenge the husband. Here too, Eugene O'Neill radically transformed the Greek myth and created a new myth on that model. He changed Medea's cold hair into the warmth of passionate love of Abbie. In O'Neill's play the wife is not real mother but a young step-mother deluged with her step-son, Medea killed her children to avenge Jason, but Abbie does so to prove her love to Eben and symbolically to avenge her husband, Ephraim. It is further noteworthy that Medea after her separation married Aegeus, Theseus's father, and at the arrival of Theseus, her step-son, she tried to kill him, and it led to her fleeing from Athens. (Mahfouz 13) Further, it is not Ephraim but Eben who proclaims the catastrophic parental curse.

Ephraim too voices God's curse on his sons. Abbie stands as an instrument of fate like Poseidon, Ephraim is left isolated among the ruins of his farms and home like Theseus who retired in the court of Lycomedes who later assassinated him.

Eugene O'Neill skips the play adroitly through melodramatic waters of greed, violence, sex, incest, adultery and infanticide by controlling various elements with the suggestions of the past which determine the present and future. Later, in the play Abbie and Eben rise above incest and greed, and face death in love. The play ends with a paradox that death and love, victory and defeat, hope and despair come hand in hand which embody O'Neill's philosophy of man's struggle against an inevitable and inescapable fate. The rich avenues of religious mythology for artistic expression fascinated Eugene O'Neill. His journey of dramatic art started with Greek tragedy- to a ritual to the Bible (the archetypal events of the Old and the New Testament). The character of Ephraim, a nineteenth century puritan, is O'Neill's distorted version of the archetypal patriarch. He is associated with Abraham who through his leadership, his vision of the Promised Land, his passionate desire for an heir, and his rejection of his son (Racey 42). Unlike Abraham he never seeks and never achieves reconciliation with his sons and he loses his heirs one by one. Ephraim is an embodiment of cruel and harsh aspect of the figure of Abraham. Frederic Carpenter opines that, "to himself he is the chosen instrument of an Old Testament God." (106). His God is similarly distorted Old Testament God, the desert God of vengeance and wrath who cannot forgive. Ephraim says;" God's hard, not easy! God's in the stones! Build my church on a rock--out o' stones an' I'll be in them!" (Batra; DUE 134)

Ephraim, the puritan father, dominates the play with his harshness. It is rather ironical that although he is seventy-five years old however, he behaves as if he would never die. His diabolical designs and self-perpetuating tyranny, self-righteousness in seeking to possess the farm become embodiment of heroism of modern man, as well as an embodiment of the hubris of the Greek tragedy (Winther 332). He desires to possess everything - the farm, the woman, a defeated son and an heir.

He is an issueless father wanting to enjoy youth and the patriarchal authoritarianism. His marriage with young Abbie, with the hope that she will give him an heir exhibits his attempts to obviate the post and negate the existence of his sons. He resents his son's umpteen attempts to appropriate the farm. Yet he adopts the Hebraic concept of genealogy according to which the father's spirit and possessions live through the progeny. He does not consider his legitimate sons from former wives as true sons. He hates them because they are not hard like him but soft like their mothers.

The play's title is built on rich Biblical mythological symbolic strain. In the Biblical sense desire is a sin, the punishment awarded to Eben and Abbie is in keeping with the Biblical tradition, for they have violated God's commandments. Therefore, Eben and Abbie had to undergo punishment and Ephraim is left alone as he is also guilty of desire, greed and Freudian sin of repression. The God is replaced by the past. Gravity of crime is aggravated by the fact that it is committed under the elms. The elms could also be considered as the statues of Aphrodite and Artemis that frame the action in Euripides' *Hippolytus*. They are female symbols who symbolize Ephraim's two late wives, and mother symbols. They seem to "protect and at the same time subdue… have their intimate contact with the life of man in the house an appalling humaneness. They brood oppressively over the house" (Batra; DUE 77). Elaborating further, "they are like exhausted women resting their sagging breasts and hands and hair on its roof, and when it rains their tears tickle down monotonously and rot on the shingles" (Batra; DUE 77).

The elms represent nature thwarted by recourse to Puritanism which is symbolized by rocks, barren houses and patriarchal figures of Ephraim. Nature emerges victorious through one of its allies, Abbie, who symbolizes warmth of love, maternity and fertility. The cows, elms and Abbie are maternal symbols. Ephraim is a hard, ruthless and domineering father. The rocks enclosing the farm symbolize the masculine strength and vigour. The play celebrates rituals as in the classical tragedy and even the play is set in spring season that synchronises with the season of ritual and festivity. The kitchen-dance and Ephraim's dancing accompanied by music to celebrate his new son's birth are in tradition with the classical tragedy's ritual. His dance and victory over the fiddler symbolize his conflict with society he says, "Ye're a sickly generation! Yer hearts air pink, not red! Yer veins is full o' mud an' water! I be the on'y man in the county!" (Batra; DUE 156). The fiddler, the young girl, and the old farmer are members of O'Neillian version of the classical chorus. They serve the playwright's expository purpose in relation with the illicit love affair of Abbie and Eben.

In the fashion of the classical tragedy Eugene O'Neill is enabled by his dexterous handling of myth to furnish retribution, Eben and Abbie are faced with God's wrath which is symbolized by their conflict in their consciences. Abbie confesses her crime of murdering "the child o' our sin" and Eben submits to having a hand in the murder. (Batra; DUE 180) Thus, O'Neill re-dramatized the classical myth and Biblical patterns in *Desire Under the Elms*.

The use of mythical patterns and symbols bestowed upon him capabilities to transmit his visualisation of life and tragedy, wherein the characters attain life and hope in their defeat and death. O'Neill grappled with the problem of man's conflicts and their inescapable consequences. It is bursting with the themes of incest, infanticide and looming fate. The trees conjure both mythology and Greek tragedy in a naturalistic setting in which characters driven solely by subconscious and primordial drives submit to their instincts and desires without any intellectual or higher order motivation.

MYTHS IN THE GREAT GOD BROWN

In *The Great God Brown*, O'Neill puts the technique of expressionism to some noble use. He uses masks to present duality of character. His fascination for the masks was enhanced by his realization that it has an affinity with the dramatic processes, and its psychological significance. O'Neill himself championed expressionism and its numerous techniques, including the use of masks. In his essay "Memoranda on Masks", exhibiting his faith in the psychological, mystical and abstract quality of the masks he believed masks to be the best solution to showcase modern man's trials and tribulations. They give its users dramatic clarity and are economic to use as it provides vent to complex mental conflicts which the study of human psychology unveils (3).

O'Neill endowed the plot, character, theme and dialogue with symbolic and mythical properties. The names and the dramatist's personae suggest mystical and mythical patterns. He used mythical names to add richness and depth. The name of Dion Anthony is symbolic and suggestive. Doris Falk eloquently explains the playwright's ideas behind Dion's name. It is formed from two words Dion that is Dionysus who is associated with creativity and St. Anthony who is associated with lifeless and sapless attitude towards life. These two different personalities are under a persistent fight that leads to mutual collapse. So, Dion Anthony becomes self-destructive as he is unable to regulate the fights, he undergoes within himself. This therefore led to a transformation from Pan like qualities to devilish Mephistophelian (101).

Dion stands for art and creativity. He is a victim of destructive forces of life- affirming creativity and life-denying aestheticism. He, along with Brown, represent a composite whole of modern man, and symbolize the man's self-destructive struggle to exist. His values of love and friendship were given a blow by the evil remarks of Brown in his childhood. He puts on the masks of the Pan later on over his spiritual, poetic and innocent self. His wish of Margaret communicating with his inner-self remains unfulfilled as she lives on surfaces. His mask gradually becomes Mephistophelian, and mocks his anguish over his alienation with his father. His fall is inevitable when he agrees to sell his talents by working for businessman Brown. It is a fall of a creative pagan before the materialistic businessman Brown. Even after death Dion's mask overpowers him to live.

Brown symbolises the forces of materialism who has no mask to begin with. But after Dion's death he wears his mask to possess Dion's wife, Margaret. He is diabolically enslaved by the mask because he has put one which bears exactness after Dion's mocking mask which puts him under the heart-rending conflict. Brown's character showcases a typical American of pre-depression era who believes in success and getting it even if it means sacrificing values of love and friendship. Brown becomes the God of Success, and exhibits full faith in the American myth of the success. No idea appeals to his imagination more than his dream of material success and self-advancement. Dion remarks about him, "He's heaven-bent for success. It is the will of Mammon!" (O'Neill 30). Brown has hollowness of consciousness, and his urge to live the stolen life of Dion by wearing his mask makes him mad. He can live no life neither of the Billy Brown, nor the creative life of Dion. His various faces bewilder him and he speculates: "Oh, how many persons in one God make up the good God Brown?" (O'Neill 84). He undergoes the terrible impact of the Satanic masks. He says, "Ugly! Hideous! Despicable! Why must the demon in me pander to cheapness—then punish me with self-loathing and life- hatred? Why am 1 not strong enough to perish or blind enough to be content" (O'Neill 84).

Eugene O'Neill as a serious playwright of his age could foresee the heinous repercussion of the nineteen twenties materialism and individualism in the character of Brown. He forecasts as early as 1926 the impending depression which would prove to be a pathetic and grotesque delusion. Cybel is an idol of Mother Earth who plays the role of both mother and mistress. She symbolizes glorious and ignominious qualities of womanhood. Eugene O'Neill observed, "Cybel is an incarnation of Cybele, the Earth mother doomed to segregation as a pariah in a world of unnatural laws but patronized by segregators who are thus themselves the first victims of their laws" (qtd. in Cole 238).

Symbolically, she represents the 'Life Force'. Her character helps in exposing corruption and viciousness of the conscience of modern men who come to her as flesh-seekers. She symbolises fertility. She is called by Dion as 'Miss Earth' (O'Neill 40). The playwright might have had in his mind the homonym 'sybil' because she preserves her sooth-saying faculties which are reminiscent of the Delphic priestess. Her yellow hair symbolizes her fertility, and towards the end it hangs down in a great mane over shoulders (Tornqvist 368). Her role changes frequently for Dion. She is his sister at a moment, and the next she becomes maternal to provide the only answer to pin his soul into every vacant diaper, and her hand is "a cool mud poultice on the string of thought" (O'Neill 40). The images of seasons, especially autumn and spring, are connected with her. Dion's love for her is moved by quietness and parental love which she offers him. Her counterpart Margaret is an "image of modern direct descendent of the Marguerite of Faust —the eternal girl- woman with a virtuous simplicity of instinct, properly oblivious to everything but the means to her end of maintaining the race" (Cole 238). Margaret with Cybel serves as the counterparts of Brown and Dion. Margaret is thrown into insignificance because of her all-consuming simplicity. She does not wear any mask like Billy Brown, lives a life of surfaces, and does not deal with inner realities.

Eugene O'Neill uses masks as symbols in this play. The characters' use masks as symbols of their ego to the outside world. They remove their masks either in isolation or in intimate group to expose their inner selves. They reveal their fears and closest feelings. Dion speaks in the Prologue about the turmoil he is undergoing regarding his behaviour that is quite submissive and introverted. He honestly accepts his love for dance, love, peace and friendship but is unable to show it as the cruel materialistic world is cajoles him to hide his creativity behind a mask which he calls his "armor" O'Neill 20-21). He articulates his inner chaos which is quoted by Savithri Subramaniam: "Why am I afraid to dance...to love.... why hide myself in self-contempt in order to understand? Why must I be ashamed of my strength, so proud of my weaknesss?" (84). Continuing furtheron, "Why must I live in a cage like a criminal, defying and hating, I who love peace and friendship?.... Why was I born without a skin, O God, that I must wear armor in order to touch or to be touched. " (84)....

Dion's words are illustrative of his bewilderment and self-contempt at wearing the mask which is constantly related with inner conflict of soul. When Brown steals Dion's mask to replace him as the lover of Margaret, he suffers from spiritual turmoil. Thus, the masks occupy an essential and important part. But at times, it becomes confusing because of their frequent changes by the characters. Kenneth Tynan, English theatre critic and writer, has castigated the playwright for employing the device of masks. Undoubtedly, the unconvincing proliferation of masks strains the credibility. Yet it can be conceded that Eugene O'Neil meant it to be interpreted in the vein of anti-realism wherein some allowance should be made to allegory and the dexterity of the artist to realize the symbolic meaning (121). Dion and Brown are infused in a single character.Cybel calls Brown, when he wears Dion's mask, as Dion Brown. They are one man, the hard-headed breadwinner, striving for emotional inner life or thwarted artist or lover seeking for material success as many facets of an individual.

When we consider the two as close associates in business and interpret the play allegorically, the intensification of Dion and Brown as one person becomes clear.Margaret loves Billy only when he wears the Pan-mask of Dion. She herself wears a mask to conceal her disillusionment. Cybel, the incarnation of natural biological sex, pities both of them. She blesses them when the two masks merge into Man. Eugene O'Neill saw the tensions of organic character Dion Brown in shuffling and arranging of the masks, suffering from divided self as a modern man. Brown remarks: "This is Daddy's bed-time secret for today: Man is born broken. He lives by mending. The grace of God is glue!" (O'Neill 89). Brown's success will be an empty halo if unaided by Dion's genius. He feels conscious of his inadequacies in designing the Temple of Man's Soul (O'Neill 65). The man Brown is submerged in the numerous public personages that he contemplated. Unlike Dion who symbolized Pan like quality, Brown worshipped only success.

The playwright exhausted the vocabulary of mask to dramatize the characters demarcated public and private selves in a highly symbolic drama which is not totally aimed at the verisimilitude of the realistic drama. The playwright filters "an ironic vision of humanity through a sieve of pitiful despair and the embellishment of the residuum with the species of ejaculation, customarily associated with dock labourers and presidents of the United States in this beautiful and majestic work" (Nathan 69). Overall, the playwright embodied typical romantic theme with modern motives and the myth of success. It illustrates the creative imagination as the basic process of romantic affirmation of man's archetypal quest from states to recognition of the existence of an organic aim and timelessness of the Ednic Time.

Eugene O'Neill went on to show that Margaret was a direct descendant of the Marguerite of Faust, "the eternal girl-woman ... properly oblivious to everything but the means to her end of maintaining the race." Cybel, he called an incarnation of the Earth Mother. Doris Falk calls Brown an aimless semi-god of the capitalized world who is making buildings but is inwardly empty (103). Eugene O'Neill, in his now famous letter to the Post, called Billy Brown, the "protagonist" of his play. Brown is sapless, lifeless and visionless businessman who is a being of shallow and artificial predetermined social grooves. Savithri Subramaniam relevantly quotes, "The visionless demi-God of our new materialistic myth - a success - building his life of exterior things, inwardly empty and resources-less, an uncreative creature of superficial preordained groves, a by-product forced aside into slack water by the main currents of life desire" (87).

Dion Anthony berates Brown and address him thus, "But to be neither creature nor creator! To exist only in her indifference! To be unloved by life! (BROWN stirs uneasily) To be merely a successful freak, the result of some snide neutralizing of life forces -a spineless cactus..." (O'Neill 61). To O'Neill, Brown represented the contemporary commercial businessman, filling himself with money rather than a soul. He saw money as sin. Dion mentions Billy Brown's original sin committed when he had hit the four-year-old Dion on the head and destroyed the sand picture, thereby giving birth to the "evil and injustice of man" (O'Neill 60). Billy must atone for that moment and also for his life-long attempt to become what he is not. He has committed sin and must suffer until cleansed. Dion Anthony who is a Christ figure will be his model as Christ was to all humankind.

Dion helps Billy by willing to give him his mask, which has been the symbol of torture and anguish, but also has the supremacy to move a human being from a state of sin to that of grace. Brown dons the mask in his need to be like Dion, and his atonement begins, and we can see at the climax that Brown is stripped of all his worldly possessions, corporeally dishevelled, pathetic in his anguish, buried symbolically in the arms of Cybel (Mother Earth), praying to be taken out of his pit of earthly hell. Finally, in his dying breath, he is mercifully allowed the glory and exaltation of facing his Maker, and the pinnacle is reached. In a sudden ecstasy at the threshold of his death, he proclaimed- "Only he that has wept can laugh! The laughter of Heaven sows earth with a rain of tears, and out of Earth's transfigured birth-pain the laughter of Man returns to bless and play again in innumerable dancing gales of flame upon the knees of God!", and he dies at the death of his utterance (O'Neill 95).

Eugene O'Neill uses mythological symbolism in *The Great God Brown* to illustrate psychology of his characters. Dion Anthony and William Billy Brown represent two opposite figures in Greek mythology, Apollo and Dionysus. Apollo was the messenger of the Gods and the presiding deity of music, medicine, and youth. Dionysus was God of vegetation and wine. In the second half of the nineteenth century, Nietzsche used the terms Apollonian and Dionysian to note the distinction between reason and culture (Apollonian), and instinct and primitiveness (Dionysian). Many authors were influenced by Nietzsche's discussion of these opposing forces. D. H. Lawrence, for example, employed Apollonian/Dionysian symbolism in his works to illustrate the theme of intellect versus instinct. Eugene O' Neill uses this tension of opposites in his representation of the relation between Billy and Dion. Billy represents the controlled intellect that is incapable of experiencing any kind of creative inspiration. Dion, whose name echoes Dionysus, symbolizes instinct and the liberation of the senses in an effort to release divine creativity.

Another Greek God, Eugene O' Neill symbolizes in his play is Pan, the pastoral God of fertility and mischief. In Greek mythology, he was depicted as sometimes merry, sometimes ill-tempered jokester with the horns and the legs of a goat. Later, he became associated with Dionysus. Dion's mask represents the figure of Pan, and when he and Billy wear it, they take on his personality. This Pan-like mask, however, takes on

Mephistophelian characteristics as Dion's artistic ambitions are continually thwarted.

When Billy takes the credit for Dion's architectural creativity, his growing sense of betrayal prompts him to condemn his friend. Yet, as the mask increases its satanic distortion, Dion's face becomes more spiritual. Here, Eugene O' Neill begins to stress more on Christian symbolism. Dion's last name, Anthony, suggests Saint Anthony, who, according to tradition, resisted every temptation the devil could devise for him. By the end Dion becomes a martyred Saint Anthony, rejecting the temptations of alcohol and the impulse to punish Billy for his betrayal of him (Students).

The American drama prior to Eugene O' Neill was detached from life and culture, though some plays were written in naturalistic and realistic vein. It sought to establish a relationship between the native drama and the culture as embodied in a myth to emphasize the representation and American character of drama after 1920. He distinctly displayed the qualities of a mythologist which were to leave a mark, though four decades later, on the newly independent Indian subcontinent writers who were still yearning for a dramatic form of self-expression that could help them discern the present with their feet firmly grounded in the mythical and enticing past.

GIRISH KARNAD: USAGE OF MYTHS

Drawing from both traditions and the modernism was Indian dramatist Girish Karnad. Girish Karnad, an accomplished actor and film director with a career spanning many decades, has written fourteen plays in Kannada, his adopted language, including *Yayati, Tughlaq, Nagamandala, Hayavadana, Agni Mattu Male* and *Taledanda* which have won him some of India's top awards and honours. Like the world drama even Indian drama was heavily seeped into realism. Girish Karnad was strictly against blatant copying of the west "living room" culture into Indian plays. He places a lot of importance on the Indian kitchen as the central area of conversation as compared to western drawing/living room. In his speech delivered at *Meet the Author* programme organized by Sahitya Akademi and the Indian International Centre in 1988 he said all the naturalistic plays in West take place "in the drawing room…the living room of the house is the central point for the individual …everything happens in the living room …not only in theatre but in society itself, it is where a person belongs". Drawing a contrast with India, he says that "in India living room is really a place where you meet guests and give them tea…The family really meets inside the kitchen or talks in the kitchen or in the eating place" (Karnad 89).

While theatre experimented with newer forms, Indian English drama performed its archaic form for many years the reason being Indian audience not eager to enjoy theatre especially, English plays (Nagarajan 1). Since, Indian living room was a site of formal cordiality. Therefore, Girish Karnad tried to break this geography of living room by giving it an Indian touch thereby revolutionizing Indian theatre and freeing it from the tentacles of the west. Vinay Dharwadker opines that post-independence era led to a rise in the search of a common Folk culture with which people could find their bearing and feel comfortable in expressing themselves. He said "Post 1960's Indian drama was Anti-realistic as opposed to realistic European drama of Ibsen, Shaw or Chekhov" (240).

Girish Karnad pioneered myth and folklore usage in Indian theatre and made widespread use of myths to highlight social ills. A strident critic of the Hindutva movement and the rise of religious fundamentalism in India, Girish Karnad focused on the misuse of myths for political purposes. Girish Karnad's hallmark has been his knack to spot apt myths from the past and place them in the contemporary scenario. As it has been noted by Prema Nandkumar, a leading literary critic, that Girish Karnad's creativity is visible in his usage of both historical legends and infusing them with scintillating techniques. Three Plays is certainly a gift for all seasons" (434). Girish Karnad grew up watching three kinds of theatre namely, The Company *Natak, Yakshagana* and the Western theatre. Having been exposed to such a wide array of performances he wrote his plays akin to Company *Natak* form and style. Girish Karnad wanted to be a poet. But, talking candidly in a speech delivered at *Meet the Author* programme organized by Sahitya Akademi and the Indian International Centre in 1988 he confessed that he was astounded to find himself writing a myth-based play in Kannada (89). The first play that Girish Karnad wrote was based on a Mahabharata myth because personally he found himself in a predicament that could best be explained via it. Coming from a traditional middle-class family and going abroad with a heavy weight of familial expectations got him writing about *Yayati*.

MYTHS IN *YAYATI*

Yayati was Girish Karnad's first play and it was written neither in English nor in his mother tongue Konkani. Instead, it was written in his adopted language Kannada. This play that chronicled the adventures of mythical characters from the *Mahabharata* was an instant success and was immediately translated and staged in several other Indian languages. Girish Karnad's *Yayati* is written in *Yakshagana* style wherein a Sutradhara enters the stage and directly address the audiences. *Yayati* opens with Sutradhara and he is addressing the audience. Being Girish Karnad's central mouthpiece, *The Sutradhara,* justifies using myth in the play, he admits that one does not turn to folklore to find resolutions or consolation but because it acts as a mirror for our fears and despair residing restlessly within a man. He admits, "It is a good way to get introduced to ourselves" (Karnad; YAYA 6). Girish Karnad opines that a myth is not an escape but an acceptance of reality. He also admits to fabricating stories he says, "But we must trust the narrative we have chosen for ourselves. Invent bits if necessary, but go on. We must relive, not a saga embedded in books, but a tale orally handed down by our grandmothers in lamp lit corners." (Karnad; YAYA 6)

Yayati uses the ancient myth from *Mahabharata* that emphasizes filial duty and responsibility and places a lot of importance upon accepting parents' wishes. Girish

Karnad gave this myth a modern twist. According to Hinduism, Yayati was the first king of *Pauravas* and the son of King *Nahusha* and his wife *Ashokasundari* daughter of *Shiva* and *Parvati*. He was *Pandava's* ancestor. Yayati had conquered the whole world and was the universal monarch or the emperor of the world. He married Devyani, Shukracharya's daughter, the priest of the demons and makes the daughter of king Vishparva, Sharmistha his mistress on her request. After hearing about his relation with Sharmishtha, Devayani complains to her father Shukracharya, who in turn curses Yayati to old age in the prime of life, but later allows him to exchange it with his son, Pooru. Yayati's son Pooru accepts his father's curse and becomes old at a young age while his father continues enjoying carnal pleasures.

B. Yadav Raju asserts that Girish Karnad has portrayed Yayati as a selfish king who longs for eternal youth and is ready to usurp his son's young age without second thoughts. Girish Karnad invests new meaning and significance for contemporary life and reality by exploring the king's motivations. In the *Mahabharata,* Yayati comprehends that desire can never be quenched as it can't be eliminated nor reduced. In the drama, Girish Karnad makes Yayati confront the horrifying consequences of not being able to relinquish desire; and through the other characters he highlights the issue of class, caste and gender coiled within a web of desire (18). Girish Karnad telescopes the entire episode of *Mahabharata* and takes artistic leverages to bring forth the recurrent theme of Indian myths wherein the parents demand sacrifices from their children. This parental demand of Indian myths is quite different from the Greek myths wherein the children are seen aggressing against their parents. The play opens with prince Pooru who comes home after many years. He has successfully completed his education in the hermitage under renowned Gurus. He marries Chitralekha. Devayani is Shukracharya's beloved daughter. When the play opens Devyani and Yayati are married. Sharmistha who is Demon King Vrishparva's daughter is Devayani's slave who makes Devayani's life miserable with her malicious comments and demonic antics. Sharmishtha disrespects Devayani as she knows that Yayati married her because he wanted to be blessed with immortality by Devayani's father. Refuting Devyani's tall claim of Yayati lusting after her, Sharmistha says, "Except that he is not lusting for you, you poor darling, he lusts for immortality. Your father's art of 'Sanjeevani'" (Karnad; YAYA 11).

Sharmishtha and Devyani's relationship is quite fraught. The *Rakshasi* girl is vicious and takes revenge on Devayani by concocting a plan to seduce not-so-innocent Yayati. She first elaborately narrates to Yayati the reason behind their love-hate relationship and then tries to commit suicide by drinking a vial of lethal poison. King Yayati tries to stop her and grabs her right hand which makes them a married couple by convention that stated that if a prince held any princess with her right hand than they were to be considered married. By this convention, Yayati makes her his queen and both of them consummate their marriage on Poorus and Chitrlekhas bed. This is a foreshadow of the coming events wherein both the father and son will exchange places. Enraged by this incident Devayani rushes to her father who curses Yayati to lose his youth and become decrepitude by night fall. However, Shukracharya gives one allowance that if Yayati wanted, he could exchange his old age with someone and take their youth from him.

Girish Karnad gives a profound vision of Yayati's character who is like the modern man. Just like Yayati, modern man in spite of enjoying life, still feels disgruntled and yearns for more. Yayati exchanges his old age with son Pooru but soon realizes how inappropriate his shallow actions are and ultimately feels alienated. Yayati feels devastating disenchantment and beseeches Pooru to take back his youth he says, "Please help me, Pooru. Take back your youth. Let me turn my decrepitude into a beginning" (Karnad; YAYA 69). Girish Karnad took the original myth and changed it. In the play Chitralekha's death opens Yayati's eyes otherwise in *The Mahabharta* Yayati doesn't realise it. As has been pointed out by B. Yadav Raju that, "Yayati forsakes his life of sensual delights only after indulging in it for a thousand years" (80).

Girish Karnad took creative leverages and confessed to having introduced Chitralekha, in his interview with Tutun Mukherjee. He admits to having created Chitralekha's character so as to lay importance on serene acceptance of Pooru and his repercussions on his wife. This made Poorus act look senseless and stupid. Sharmistha and Chitralekha are the ones who wake Yayati out of his selfish slumber. They also aren't afraid to act and own up their destiny without worrying about consequences. (Mukherjee 31). Through Yayati, Girish Karnad showcases modern man's dilemma and his constant state of flux wherein he feels incomplete. Myths highlight modern life absurdities. Girish Karnad makes myths his vehicles to comment on modern man's predicaments and problems.

MYTHS IN HAYAVADANA

Girish Karnad does not draw heavily from the myths but moulds them and supplements with his imagination. Hayavadana's plot is partly derived from Kathasaritsagara, an ancient stories collection in Sanskrit and partly from Thomas Mann's retelling of the story in the Transposed Head. M.K.Naik clarifies the difference between the two. He says that Mann's focus was to stress the ironic impossibility of uniting perfectly the spirit and the flesh in human life while Girish Karnad tried to highlight existential problem and the metaphysical agony of human beings (Naik 137).

Mann has given the Sanskrit tale a mock-heroic description. Mann takes the moral problem of whether the body is superior or the head is supreme but uses it to ridicule the philosophy that holds the head to be superior. Mann argues that destiny is what matters as nature imposes limits. Jose George comments that Girish Kamad's trend setting play *Hayavadana* strikes a significant note by exploring the dramatic potential of the historical myths, folktales and traditions" (213). *Hayavadana* is inspired by *Vetal Panchavimshati* that consist of twenty-five stories narrated to King *Vikramaditya* by a celestial spirit *Vetal*. It is a collection of tales consisting story within stories. It was written in Sanskrit one of its oldest edited series is found in the twelfth book of *Kathasaritsagara* written by Somdeva. In the story the legendary king *Vikramaditya* promises a sage that he will capture *Vetal*, who hangs upside-down from a tree and inhabits and animates dead bodies. King *Vikramaditya* faces many difficulties in bringing the *Vetal* to the sage. Each time *Vikramaditya* tries to capture the *Vetal,* he tells a story that ends with a riddle. If *Vikramaditya* cannot answer the question correctly, the vampire consents to remain in captivity. If the king knows the answer but still keeps quiet, then his head shall burst into thousand pieces. And if King *Vikramaditya* answers the question correctly, the vampire would escape and return to his tree. He knows the answer to every question; therefore, the cycle of catching and releasing the vampire continues twenty-four times (Somadeva 14). When *Vikramaditya* puts *Vetal* back on his shoulders, he starts with one of his stories: Once upon a time there lived a washer man named *Devashish*. One day, he was washing clothes by the bank of a river where he saw a very beautiful lady, and he instantly fell in love. He enquired and found out that she was a Brahmin's daughter who lived in a nearby village and her name was *Madhusundari*. *Devashish* went to meet *Madhusundari's* parents and asked them for her hand. They readily agreed and soon *Devashish* was married to *Madhusundari*. A few months went by happily. On *Dussehra, Madhusundari's* brother came to invite his sister and brother-in-law to their place. *Devashish* agreed and the three of them started their journey to *Madhusundari's* home.

On the way they happened to pass by the temple of *Durga Devi*. Her brother wanted to pray to the Goddess, and went to the temple. But when he came near the idol of the Goddess, he was overwhelmed with emotions, and he decided to cut off his head and offer it to the goddess. When the young man did not come back, *Madhusundari* sent her husband to check what the matter was. On seeing the dead body of his brother-in-law, *Madhusundari's* husband also decided to offer his own head to the goddess and severed his head with a knife. After some time, *Madhusundari* herself went inside the temple to check. She was devastated to see both her brother and husband lying on the ground. She wanted to take her own life and begged the goddess to give her the same brother and husband in the next life. The Goddess was pleased and stopped her from killing herself.

She asked her to join their heads and bodies so as to grant life. Out of excitement, she attached her husband's head to her brother's body and her brother's head to her husband's body. When she realized her mistake, she looked at the Goddess for help but the Goddess said that it was impossible to exchange the heads. *Vetal* stopped *Vikramaditya* and asked him, "Who among the two is *Madhusundari's* husband?

Vikramaditya replied with a lot of thought, "The head is the most essential part of the human body, so *Madhusundari's* husband should be the body that carries her husband's head." As soon as *Vikramaditya* had finished his answer, *Vetal* disappeared back to the tree" (Somdeva 138).

This tale forms the basis of Girish Karnad's play. He starts with a puja to *Ganesha,* as the Bhagavata asks *Ganesha* to bless the performance that he and the company are about to perform. Then he places the audience in the setting of the play,

Dharmapura, and begins to introduce the central characters. The first is Devdatta who is a Brahmin's son outshines the other pundits and poets of the kingdom. The second is Kapila who is an iron-smith's son who is skilled at physical feats of strength. The two are the closest of friends. As the Bhagavata sets up the story, there is a scream of terror offstage. An actor runs onstage screaming that he has seen a man with a horse's head and human voice. Bhagavata doesn't believe him, and even when the creature Hayavadana enters, the Bhagavata thinks it is a mask and attempts to pull off Hayavadana's head.

Upon realizing it is his real head, the Bhagavata listens as Hayavadana explains his origin. He is a princess's and a celestial being's son in horse form, and he yearns to become a full man. The Bhagavata suggests him to go to *Kali's* temple, as she grants anything anyone asks for. Hayavadana goes to the temple, hopeful that *Kali* will be able to change his head to a human head.

In the meanwhile, Bhagavata returns to the play. He begins to sing, explaining that the two heroes start to love a girl and forgot themselves. Meanwhile, a female chorus sings in the background about the nature of love. Devadatta and Kapila enter. Devadatta explains his love for

Padmini, explaining that he would sacrifice his arms and his head if he could marry her. Kapilaat first makes fun of Devadatta but then sees how much his friend is affected by Padmini. He agrees to find out her name and where she lives. Kapila goes to the street where Padmini lives and begins to knock on the door. When Padmini opens the door to her home, Kapila is immediately love-struck. Padmini questions him about his wants, outwitting him as he tries to come up with reasons why he is there. He eventually confesses that he is there to woo her for Devadatta. Kapila says to himself that Padmini really needs a man of steel, and that Devadatta is too sensitive for someone as quick as Padmini. Bhagavata reveals that Devadatta and Padmini were quickly married, and that all three remained friends. The story then jumps forward six months, when Padmini is pregnant with a son, and the three friends are meant to go on a trip to Ujjain together. Devadatta expresses jealousy that Padmini seems to have some affection for Kapila, which Padmini denies. She is willing to cancel the trip in order to spend more time together, but when Kapila arrives, ready to leave, Padmini changes her mind and decides to go, much to Devadatta's dismay.

As the three of them travel together, Padmini remarks how well Kapila drives the cart. She points out a tree with the flower, and Kapila rushes off to grab flowers for her. Padmini remarks to herself how muscular Kapila is, and Devadatta sees Padmini watching him with desire. When they pass *Rudra* and *Kali's* temple, Devadatta is reminded of his old promise and sneaks away to cut off his head. Kapila goes to look for him, and upon discovering Devadatta's headless body is struck with grief. He decides to cut off his head as well. Padmini begins to get worried about the two men and goes after them. She sees their two headless bodies on the ground and attempts to commit suicide. The Goddess *Kali* stops her and tells her she will revive the men if Padmini places their heads on their bodies. Padmini, in her excitement, accidentally switches the two heads. The two men revive: one with Devadatta's head and Kapila's body, and the other with Kapila's head and Devadatta's body. At first, the three of them are amused by the mix-up, but when they try to return home, they discover issues. Each man believes that Padmini is his wife. Devadatta's head claims that the head rules the body, and so she is his wife. Kapila's head argues that his hand accepted hers at the wedding ceremony, and that the child she is carrying came from his body. Padmini is aghast, but decides to go with Devadatta's head. Kapila does not return with them.

As the second act opens, Padmini and Devadatta are happier than they have ever been. She loves this newfound strength in Devadatta and wait for their child to be born. They buy two dolls for their son. The dolls speak to the audience and reveal that over time, Devadatta's new, strong body begins to revert to its old form. He and Padmini fight over how to treat their son, as she believes that Devadatta coddles him. The dolls tell the audience that Padmini begins to dream of Kapila. When the dolls begin to show signs of wear, Padmini asks Devadatta to get new ones and goes to show her son the forest. As Padmini travels through the woods, she discovers Kapila living there. He has regained his strength, just as Devadatta has lost his. He explains how difficult it was to let go off her thoughts and make peace with life and accept that he is Kapila. Devadatta returns with the dolls and tries to find Padmini in the woods. He discovers her with Kapila, and the men decide to kill each other to put an end to the struggle between their heads and their bodies. After they are killed, Padmini decides to perform *Sati,* throwing herself on their funeral pyre. The Bhagavata explains that Padmini was, in her own way, a devoted wife.

Seconds later an actor comes onstage saying that he saw a horse walking down the street singing the national anthem. The first actor also enters, with a young boy in tow. The boy is very serious, and does not speak, laugh, or cry. It is revealed the child is Padmini's son. At that point, Hayavadana returns. He explains that he had asked *Kali* to make him complete, but instead of making him a complete human, she has made him a complete horse. Padmini's son begins to laugh at Hayavadana, and the two sing together.

Hayavadana, still wishes to rid himself of his human voice, and the boy encourages him to laugh. As Hayavadana laughs more and more, his laughter turns into a horse's neigh, and he thus becomes a complete horse. The Bhagavata concludes the story by marvelling at the mercy of

Ganesha, who has fulfilled the desires of Hayavadana and the young boy. He says that it is time to pray, and Padmini, Devadatta, and Kapila join in thanking the Lord.

The play is unique in several ways as Girish Karnad wrote the play partly as a reaction against Western theatrical conventions; he begins by placing the audience directly within the Indian culture and religion that permeate his play. The play also introduces element of hybridity as it is a mixture of Indian and western myths.

Hayavadana who is half horse and half human is a similar character found in Greek myths called Centaur. *Ganesha* is the first of many beings with a mismatched head and body to appear in the play. With the play's human characters, hybridity is associated with a state of incompleteness, but the Bhagavata argues here that divine beings do not have that same deficiency; their perfection is incomprehensible to mortals. The play is a successful example of the "theatre of roots" movement in India. This movement began after India gained independence from Britain in 1947, and playwrights began to move away from Western dramatic conventions in favour of using regional languages and theatrical forms in their plays. *Hayavadana* is written in the regional Indian language Kannada and uses elements of Indian *Yakshagana* and *Natak Theatre.* Karnad uses these various theatrical forms within his play to argue that the idea of India as a unified nation is a construction, and that modern Indian culture is in fact made up of many diverse traditions.

Girish Karnad's play brings to forefront the problem of identity in a domain of twisted relationships. When the play opens, Devadutta and Kapila are the closest of friends- one mind and one heart, as described by the Bhagvata. Devdatta is a man of intellect, Kapila a man of the body. Their world gets complicated when Devdatta marries Padmini. Kapila loves Padmini and she too starts swaying towards him. The friends kill themselves and Padmini transposes their heads, giving Devdatta Kapila's body and Kapila Devdatta's. The result of confusing identities reveals the ambiguous nature of human personality. Devdatta, actually the head on Kapila starts behaving differently from what he was before. But ever so gradually he changes into his former self, so does Kapila, but there is a difference. Devdatta stopped writing poetry and Kapila is haunted by the memories in Devdatta's body. Padmini after the exchange of heads thought she had the best of both men however, gradually she gets disillusioned. She understands but is unable to change the situation in which three of them are. A duel leaves both the friends dead and brings the puzzling story to an end. Nothing is shown as tragic by Girish Karnad as death was their only solution since they were caught in the absurdity of life.

Girish Karnad uses the combination of myths and the dramatic devices to create a story reflecting the real dilemma in love to choose over mind or soul.

Although in our Indian context myths are related to religion, Girish Karnad is only interested in the mythical side of it. Moreover, the elements of myth and history are common to most audiences in India. Most myths have a strong emotional significance, the audiences have set responses towards them, and Girish Karnad likes to play on that. In this regard, Indian playwrights are placed in an advantageous position compared to western playwrights. For, they face the tediousness and risk of taking the situation from an alien culture and make it acceptable to Christian audience. As for instance, the division of labour based on the individual's capacity for intellectual and physical labour, and the belief that a woman can only live in the society with her husband and with none other and that she should mount the pyre on the death of her husband, as shown in *Hayavadana*, are or were, some of the basic attitudes of people which Girish Karnad refuses to reform or comment upon directly. Yet, he manages to offer an alternate perspective to the audience. Girish Karnad makes certain changes in the original myth. For example, he changes the names of the characters. Girish Karnad believes that folk conventions like chorus, music, mixing of human and non-human worlds permit a side- by-side exhibition of alternate points of view. Thus, the myth acquires new dimensions in the creative hands of Girish Karnad, and the play unfolds rich strands of meaning. As M. K. Naik says, "*Hayavadana* presents the typical existential anguish, but does not stop at the existential despair" (140). Naik comments that his works suggest a way out through integration in an irrational and absurd world. Finally, Girish Karnad's use of *Indianised* expressions and symbolism deserves mention as they highlight myths. The scene in where Kapila goes to woo Padmini for Devadatta is a scene that is borrowed from older stories told in Indian theatre, but a modern spin is put on it by having the woman outwit the man instead of the other way around. He uses Indian myths to express his dramatic theme instead of borrowing, ideas, themes and technique of western drama. On the western stage drawing room is the place of action however, in India a kitchen is where pertinent discussions are held and important decisions taken. Girish Karnad revived Indian theatre with his usage of Indian myths. He adopted the myths and adapted them with respect to the present times and reworked folk narratives that ultimately acted as a fountain of rejuvenation for Indian drama in English. This new dramatic form takes plots, themes and ideas from traditional forms and weave them into his plays. This gives a fresh perspective to his plays and reinvigorates them to reflect contemporary socio-economic and political situation in a subtle and well-defined way.

MYTHS IN NAGAMANDALA

Nagamandala is a play which is fully related to the folktales of the South India. It includes the snake myth of Karnataka. Girish Karnad heard two folktales from his fellow

A.K. Ramanujan. *Nagamandala* won Sahitya Akademi Award for Girish Karnad. These folk tales were usually recounted by older women in the family to children while they were being fed their dinner in the kitchen or before sleeping. Although the tales were children focused however, they served as parallel system of communication among the family's women. They also show how a woman understand and comprehends her reality and the subjugating patriarchal themes of the established texts. These orally transmitted tales also show the nature of tales. These stories are independent of their teller and have a life of their own as they are passed down from one generation to other. The story told by women is like a daughter that is to be married off just like a tale that is to be told and passed on.

These tales have their origin in Indian tradition and rich culture. Girish Karnad borrows heavily from this rich cultural source of regional and Sanskrit classics and weaves a modern story out of them. In *Nagamandala*, Rani is married to Appanna who keeps her locked in the house and comes only for lunch during the day. Rani is akin to a newly married girl in a large joint family who gets to see two sides of her husband. One wherein he is a strict family man and other of a lover during night. This is visible from Rani's eyes as relation pattern that blooms during the night but is nectar less during the day and in front of others. Appanna has no family so the empty house is a parallel to a joint family. The prominent myth used in the drama *Nagamandala* is *nagas* or Snakes, who had a high status in Hindu mythology. The word *naga* stands for deity in Sanskrit and *Pali*. It is commonly found in Hinduism and Buddhism. This also stands for a name of tribe in India. Snakes are known to cast off its skin and in Indian culture symbolize rebirth, death and mortality. All over India snakes are worshipped. In this regard, M. Sarat Babu opines that Mandala can be termed as a "tantric concept indicating inner concentration, a source of energy". He says, "Naga-Mandala is a magic religious ritual involving Naga, the snake-god of Hindus who grants the wishes of the devotees, especially the wish for fertility". He goes on to elaborate that in the play, all the wishes of Rani which are not even expressed by her openly are granted by Naga which helps her metamorphoses into a confident and strong character. She is cured of her frigidity, gets a devoted husband, her husband's concubine becomes a lifelong servant-maid for her; she begets a good son. Besides all, Naga, in addition, makes Appanna's heart fertile with love and affection for his wife. Above all, Mr. Babu, at a higher level of symbolism, declares that "Naga represents a cultural leader who brings about a socio-cultural reform" (248).

In India snakes are considered sacred and if somebody kills them by mistake, they are cremated like humans. Celibate priestess carries Naga pictures during yearly parades. They play prominent roles in various legends like *Shesha* on whom the Hindu God, *Vishnu* does yoga *nidra*. *Vasuki* is considered the king of *nagas*. *Kaliya* poisoned the river *Yamuna* where he lived. *Krishna* defeated *Kaliya* and made him leave *Yamuna*.

Manasa is the queen of snakes. *Ashtika* is half Brahmin and half *naga*. Even the Hindu God Shiva is seen wearing a snake around his neck. Pranav Joshipura comments on the significance of snakes in the play, he says that it is significant to note that "the title of the play comes not from any human character, but from a snake-Naga. The story of the Cobra suggests that the play not merely dramatizes the folktales in modern interpretations, it also implies a deeper meaning atvarious levels". He goes on to elaborate that in our Hindu mythology, "the Naga represents several images. In South India, many houses have their own shrine which is often a grove reserved for snakes, consisting of trees, festooned with creepers, situated in a corner of the garden" (258).

Nagas play an important roles in many mythologies because of their perceived quality of being both familiar and exotic. The serpent or snake or *naga* is considered as one of the most pervasive symbols. The word is derived from Latin *serpens*, a crawling animal or snake. Snakes signify both good as well evil and do not have eyelids which implies that they are reasonable and intelligent and yet humans can't decipher their movements and thinking. They are symbolic of therapeutic and transformational qualities. They also signify fertility and regarded as immortals because they renew themselves by shedding their skin. *Nagas* or Snakes are also considered to be immortal as they form a circle while they are shedding their skins and when they coil, they form spirals. Circles and spirals signify eternity.

In classical myths snakes were the guardians of the underworld since they lived underground in cracks and holes, they were also considered to be messengers of the underworld because they acted as a bridge between upper and lower world.

Nagamandala deals with a newly married girl Rani, who had the most loved childhood. Being married to a man Appanna who locks her up for the entire day to keep her away from the public gaze. Pranav comments, "The name Appanna means 'any man' and is a way to comment on any man who tries to enforce chastity on his wife, while he himself indulges in extra-marital relationships" (260). The man representing the patriarchy makes the woman the sufferer of his unjustified dominance as she is locked up in the house throughout the day. When Kurudavva Appanna's mother's friend finds out about Rani she gifts her magical roots. She persuades Rani to use her magical roots in order to cajole her husband in loving her. Unfortunately, Rani gets frightened on seeing the red colour of the boiling roots and decides to throw it away inside the ant hill where the *naga* lives. The roots cast a spell on him and he becomes smitten by Rani.

Naga being conscious of his appearance as a snake takes the form of Appanna and enters Rani's room every night. Everything goes on smoothly until Appanna discovers Rani's pregnancy. He physically abuses her. He threatens her to complain against her to the elders. The same night when *naga* visits her, he looks guilty of the actions her husband has committed. He informs her to undergo the snake chastity test. The next day when Rani takes the oath that ever since she has come into this village, she has held in her hand only two, her husband and that *naga*. Rani passes the chastity test and the villagers declare that her to be a goddess and ensure that Appanna takes care of her and the child. After years one day the *naga* while remembering his love for Rani decides to visit her. When he goes into her room, he becomes jealous of the sight of Rani sleeping with her husband and decides to kill Rani with his venom. But the very next moment he realizes that killing his Rani will be of no avail instead he decided to hide himself in the long locks of Rani.

The story of *naga* residing in the locks of Rani is similar to the Greek myth of Gorgon Medusa. In Greek Myth Medusa was considered supreme snake woman whose gaze could turn flesh into stone. These snake women were called Gorgons in Greek myths. Medusa who loved Poseidon and met him in the temple of Athena and was cursed by her. Athena turned her beautiful hair into snakes that made her appearance ghastly.

She looked terrible and turned her spectators into stones. Both the myth and the story symbolize an act of turning the head as an abode of snakes reflecting of an act that should have been avoided in the past like Medusa loving Poseidon and Rani loving *naga*. This play signifies the male difficulty to trust and love women. It also depicts the way men and women socialize in Indian society where marriage is more of a first experience of sex and love for the most people. Girish Karnad explains the deplorable status of women by juxtaposing myths and reality.This is a subtle yet covert way of dealing with forbidden themes and taboos.

Myths and folk tales create a safety valve for Girish Karnad to express and evaluate an unacceptable topic through various perspectives. These act as a smokescreen for the writer to discuss and comment upon such topics. One can camouflage one's comment on the present social and political conditions with these adaptations. Girish Karnad, of course, became one of the fulcrums of that resurgent spirit in a very short time. Girish Karnad's strident public positions on liberal traditions, communal harmony and cultural diversity that we became familiar with later perhaps had its formative embedding in his consciousness, so to say, in Sirsi. It is these ghosts, gliding in his imagination that perhaps entered his historical and mythological plays, which invariably have a combination of existential and psychological thesis as an underpinning. This holds true for Girish Karnads play *Yayati*, of the transposition in *Hayavadana* or the splintered personality in *Nagamandala*.

Eugene O'Neill and Girish Karnad have used Myths to highlight plight of man and also showcase that the contemporary peaks through the veil of past. Myths highlight and universalise man's predicaments. The contemporary role played by Myths is brought to light by Pankaj K. Singh and Jaidev:

> Seldom ideologically neutral, myths are constructed, sacralized, and disseminated for legitimizing certain power-filled practices, attitudes and ways of seeing.

Often, they are aimed at 'naturalizing' and even 'divinizing' a particular world- view. Like history, they are not easy to disown, even when they harm people. For without them, one feels culturally impoverished, strongly weightless; and yet; with them, one feels oppressed. (3)

II
THE IDENTITY QUESTION: EUGENE O'NEILL AND GIRISH KARNAD

Eugene O'Neill and Girish Karnad, as playwrights, have delved deep into the complexities of human identity, exploring the multifaceted nature of individual and collective selves. Both playwrights engage with the quest for identity, addressing themes of self-discovery, cultural inheritance, and the negotiation of societal expectations. Through their works, O'Neill and Karnad offer profound insights into the existential struggles individuals face in their search for a sense of self.

Eugene O'Neill's plays often delve into the existential crises arising from societal pressures, cultural conflicts, and personal struggles, highlighting the multifaceted dimensions of human identity. In his seminal work *Long Day's Journey into Night*, O'Neill explores the complexities of family dynamics and the impact of familial relationships on shaping individual identities. According to Thomas S. Hischak, a renowned theatre scholar, "O'Neill's plays often delve into the tragic aspects of human existence, exploring themes of self-discovery and the formation of identity under the weight of familial and societal pressures" (Hischak 275).

Similarly, Girish Karnad's works also grapple with questions of identity, particularly within the Indian context. In his play *Tughlaq*, Karnad portrays the eponymous historical figure, Muhammad bin Tughlaq, who embarks on a quest for identity and legitimacy as a ruler. As Aniket Chakraborty observes, Karnad's *Tughlaq* explores the complex negotiation between personal desires and political responsibilities, shedding light on the fluidity and fragility of identities. Karnad's plays often feature characters who navigate the complexities of cultural and social identities, reflecting the challenges individuals face in reconciling personal aspirations with societal expectations.

In both O'Neill and Karnad's works, the quest for identity is intricately connected to cultural and historical contexts. O'Neill draws on mythic elements and universal narratives to probe the construction of individual identities, while Karnad incorporates Indian folklore and history to explore the negotiation of personal and collective selves. Nidhi Gupta, in her study on Karnad's *Taledanda,* notes that the play presents the quest for identity against the backdrop of historical and mythological references, challenging conventional notions of identity and emphasizing the fluid nature of human existence.

Moreover, both playwrights examine the impact of societal and cultural pressures on shaping individual identities. O'Neill's characters often grapple with the expectations imposed by societal norms and familial legacies. The characters in his plays, such as those in *A Long Day's Journey into Night*, confront the tension between societal expectations and personal desires, struggling to define their authentic selves within the confines of societal norms. Similarly, Karnad's plays feature characters who navigate the intricacies of cultural conflicts and traditions, highlighting the challenges individuals face in reconciling their personal identities with societal expectations.

In the works of both O'Neill and Karnad, the quest for identity is a recurring theme that reflects the universal human struggle to define oneself amidst complex social, cultural, and historical contexts. Through their exploration of identity, these playwrights invite audiences to reflect on their own journeys of self-discovery and the intricate interplay between personal desires, societal expectations, and cultural inheritances.

Identity is a set of personal and behavioural characteristics which defines an individual belonging to a particular group. It is defined by the race, ethnicity, religion, language, and culture to which an individual belongs, distinguishes them from other groups, and forms their understanding and pride about their self-identity. However, individuals may be in possession of various identities because of geographical migration and mobility from one social sect to another. A person's uniqueness and distinctiveness is the outcome of the identity he chooses.

The identities that the writer portrays through the various characters are a matter of complex analysis. A person's identity can be determined by their self-conception, social presentation and the way they behave within a civilization. The term identity is loaded with meanings, values, and prejudices. It originated from the Latin word 'idem' which literally meant 'sameness' that comes from the notion of something always being itself. Human beings cannot identify themselves completely with others, individuals as well as institutions as the social structures are different at different places and they too are unstable. The identity of any individual is created by their own perceptions of the world surrounding them. It can be based on the religion, race, and class, economic and social status of family along with the cultural and religious beliefs shared by the society in which an individual leads a life. This identity may be either a group identity or an individual identity. Identity is to be assessed in terms of an individual, as member of family, of social community, of his race, his religion, his gender, his social and economic class. It ranges from a single individual's identity to the ethnic identity. Identity suggests our thoughts and feelings, our psychic presence, our place of habitation, and even our longings, dreams and desires. The individual identity, like the national identity, is formed through a series of random and frequently bizarre associations.

The Oxford English Dictionary defines identity as the quality or condition of being the same in substance, composition, nature, properties or essential sameness or oneness (1). It is the recognition of self-existence or at least one trait of it which relates an individual with his/her group, his/her class, race, religion, or his or her nation. It is the consciousness an individual has for his role in the society or outside the society. Stuart Hall, a Cultural theorist and Sociologist, talks about modern time identity. According to Hall, "Identities are never unified and in late modern times, increasingly fragmented and fractured; never singular but multiply constructed across different, other intersections and antagonistic, discourse, practices, and positions" (4). The concept of self raises some introspections such as Who am I? How can I find out my original identity? Or how do I maintain my real identity? Identity is a projection of an individual's self. This self-image modifies, alters and transform self-identity. An individual's identity is embedded in one's culture, and therefore isolation from one's culture leads to loss of one's social and cultural identity. The impulse to associate oneself with an identity encourages one to pursue identity.

Across several forms of literature, identity as a theme is important because characters work as the basis to a text and shape a plot. No matter what point in history a text is written, it is always important for readers to scrutinize a character's identity and consider why they are the way they are and why they behave the way they behave, thus grasping a more thorough understanding of the overall content. Literary writing explores certain phases of life, and among these aspects are the relation between the individual and the community not only in social but also in psychological terms of isolation of the individual.

Thus, it is important as a reader to contemplate the contextual background of a literary text because it is this that determines what would have influenced the norms of behaviour and therefore, a strong indication of why a writer would construct their characters with their idiosyncrasies and quirks. Furthermore, the construction of identity may be influenced by stereotypical views of a character's gender or culture.

Identity is a strong premise in many literary texts because a writer must always construct several identities to achieve interesting characters. So, in literature, identity is important in two ways. It helps writers to reflect their own identity in their works. Secondly, it helps the writer to sketch characters which may be different from writer's personality. Writers have always projected their identities in their work, but the development of psychological theories of personality in twentieth century provided authors with new concepts about how identities are shaped. Psychiatrists and psychologists such as Sigmund Freud, Carl Jung, Erik Erikson, and Abraham Maslow created concepts that altered how modern literature is written and judged. Knowingly or unknowingly, most modern writers use psychological concepts, or popular interpretations of such concepts, in developing a character's motivations and behaviours. Similarly, critics and biographers often judge a writer's motivations and behaviours in the same way.

The existential challenge of belonging and establishing an identity has plagued many in the literary world. Both are complex issues that have multifarious interpretations of race, ethnicity, religion and politics. Writers who are better attuned to the intricacies of such issues simultaneously create and interpret an impression of belonging and identity. Thus, the state of identity often leads to confusion due to which sense of alienation and exile grips one's psyche. It is a universal phenomenon and fact that identity is essential to any individual. The inherent ability to assert one's identity leads an individual to define themselves in terms of present times and also seek a rationale behind it. Literature of any location expresses the quest for identity of its people. This quest provides the sense of belongingness and meaningful existence. Such sense is not completely conscious or unconscious. It is a mental process in which a person goes through various questions, confusions and tries to reach at a conclusion that is known as his crisis period. Gleason has pointed out that the current usage of the word "identity" has evolved mainly from the concept of an "identity crisis" given by famous psychoanalyst Erik Erikson (912).

The dictionary meaning of "identity crisis" is "the condition of being uncertain of one's feelings about oneself, especially with respect to character, goals, and origins…" (Webster 1). The term 'crisis' in the context is a turning point or a crucial moment in one's life that leads the person to awaken from ignorance and to proceed towards wisdom of his own self. It is considered inevitable in the growth of an individual's identity. The writer presents the hero as an individual caught in the world around him, looking for his salvation either by escaping from it or by committing to its codes. There is a constant scuffle in mind of what an individual is, and the austere reality of what he attains, what he professes and what he practises, what he really is and what he would like to be taken for. This has crumbled his life leaving an insidious effect on his inner being. The injuries inflicted and the scars left on his psyche make him apprehend only of his helplessness. Painfully sentimental of his precarious position, man experiences severe limitations arising out of randomness and alienation.

This chapter explores the alienation, isolation and identity crisis confronted by various characters like Yank, Abbie, Ephraim, Brown, Dion, Devadutta, Kapila, Rani, Chitralekha, Pooru to name a few. Although Eugene O'Neill and Girish Karnad belong to two farthest social milieus, the attributes, the isolation, and the quest to find oneself and how their characters tackle themselves are similar. The characters suffer because of their sociological reasons, which cramp their spirits, thwart their ambitions and frustrate their designs to get elation. They are tactfully crafted to include deep inner problems, timidity and skewed thinking. These characters design their image of the self so as to adjust to the outside world. This leads to a conflict between the designed self and the inner real self which is unfathomable and inscrutable. They live away from the reality and have an illusory world of their own. "Who am I?" the question sounds philosophical but shakes you out of your slumber. Numbed by the cacophony of multiple noise and mechanical lifestyle, the much valuable finer elements of life are lost and it becomes too late when realisation sets in. At the end you lose your own identity in trying to gain one.

EUGENE O'NEILL: QUEST FOR IDENTITY

Identity crisis is a prominent theme in Eugene O'Neill's plays, as his characters grapple with inner conflicts, societal expectations, and the search for their true selves. O'Neill's exploration of identity crisis sheds light on the complexities of human existence and the struggle to reconcile personal desires with external pressures. Several of his plays vividly depict characters experiencing profound turmoil and questioning their identities.

In *Long Day's Journey into Night*, one of O'Neill's most acclaimed works, the Tyrone family members confront their individual identity crises. The play portrays the Tyrone family's struggle with addiction, illness, and the weight of their past. Each character, from the aging actor James Tyrone to his sons Jamie and Edmund, grapples with personal demons and battles to define their true selves. As Bhawna Singh remarks, "The play captures the essence of an identity crisis, as the characters are haunted by their pasts, burdened by their present circumstances, and uncertain about their futures" (Singh 153).

Another play by O'Neill that delves into the theme of identity crisis is *The Iceman Cometh*. Set in a bar populated by disillusioned and trapped individuals, the play explores the characters' desperate search for meaning and identity. The inhabitants of the bar, including the protagonist Hickey, confront their self-delusions and face the harsh reality of their lives. Each character grapples with the question of who they truly are and whether they can escape the cycle of self-deception. This relentless exploration of identity crisis in The Iceman Cometh showcases O'Neill's deep understanding of human struggles and the complexities of personal identity.

In addition to these plays, O'Neill's works like *A Moon for the Misbegotten* and *A Touch of the Poet* also delve into the theme of identity crisis. These plays present characters who are torn between their aspirations, societal expectations, and their past mistakes. The protagonists, Josie Hogan and Con Melody respectively, wrestle with their self-worth, battling feelings of guilt, shame, and the fear of being defined by their past actions. O'Neill explores the profound impact of personal choices on shaping one's identity and the struggle to break free from the chains of self-doubt.

Through these plays, O'Neill captures the essence of identity crisis by delving into the depths of human psyche and portraying the internal conflicts individuals face. His characters' struggles resonate with audiences, as they reflect the universal quest for self- understanding and the challenges of defining one's identity in a complex and often unforgiving world.

Eugene O'Neill's tragic vision transcends time and space. In delineating the misery of modern man he projects an image of a man who has eternally tolerated, not because of his pride but because of failure to realize his ideal to fulfil his dream and to live life on his own terms. Eugene O'Neill did not rely on fantasy or farfetched effects for his passionate search for the meaning in life, which had been utterly ignored by his predecessors, but something that placed him among the most outstanding writers of the twentieth century. The quest for identity for a better understanding of man is a subject that is found in the great tragedies of the world and is as gripping today as it was in the times of the Greek playwrights or the Elizabethans times. All these characteristics heralded Eugene O'Neill into a visionary writer rather than a psychological one.

Eugene O'Neill's plays attempt to illuminate as well as reflect the condition and predicament of man, revealing the areas of darkness and tension in modern man's consciousness. He believes that man suffers from a sense of alienation in this world; he finds himself completely isolated in a spiritually sterile universe, and therefore he cannot have a sense of harmony. His plays provide a study of the national character. Exactly what Eugene O'Neill thought of the national character was stated concisely in an interview in 1946 wherein he said: "...the growth of America - that America, given the most, of any nation, instead of becoming the greatest country in the world, is the greatest failure" (Variety 22). Commenting on America's spiritual hollowness, he accuses that "Spiritually it tried the old everlasting game of trying to possess its own soul by possessing something out of it, ...and lost both...." (22).

Eugene O'Neill's characters are in a constant state of flux as they are deeply engrossed in the search to find their identity and define themselves. Nature works in mysterious ways to limit a man's existence and shape it in its own magical ways. Modern man is viewed as a rootless being who is uprooted from his spiritual self and his past. He is always in a quest to find his bearings. This quest requires them to locate themselves in the cosmos and find remedy in nature. Eugene O'Neill considered his work to reflect and project the America's lost soul. Having a keen interest in finding the harmony of art and life, Eugene O'Neill pursued this theme to search meaning and beauty in difficulties of life. He drafted spiritual and artistic characters. Their struggles and sacrifices go down the drain because they ask more from life than it can offer. Their thirst for identity only makes them divided between a falsehood of what they might be and what the society enforces upon them.

Eugene O'Neill's *The Hairy Ape* is a play which considers the strain of a mighty stoker named Yank. The struggle is with himself, his own past and his attempt to belong. *Desire Under Elms* is a modern version of *Hippolytis's* story. It portrays the affairs of a stepmother with her stepson. In *The Great God Brown*, O'Neill has sought to exhibit man's aspirations in a vibrant lyrical style. The device of wearing a mask is important to the action. There is the opposition of the mask and the real face in the play.

IDENTITY CRISIS IN *THE HAIRY APE*

The Hairy Ape is a play that handles with artistic mastery Yank's story. He represents everyman, a proletariat, a symbol of a man who is brutalized by industrial machinery and trapped by his idealized steel-self, which he presumes to be power. He presents an adverse view of the highly evolved mechanized America through his protagonist. It questions the very existence of human beings and their purpose; it wakes us from our slumber of a mechanical lifestyle. In the story Yank, the hairy ape, thinks that he owns the entire world of the ship and is accountable for an important task of making the ship move forward. He is devastated when his existence is questioned and finds everything to be an illusion. The Play examines the loss of identity of a white man in a dehumanized industrialized habitat. The environment is instrumental in reducing everyman represented in Yank to a fragmented being.The genesis of Eugene O'Neill's *The Hairy Ape*, was the suicide of Driscoll, a Liverpool Irishman during the playwright's brief stay at Jimmy's house. This expressionistic play is an honest attempt to examine the reasons behind Driscoll's suicide. He pins down the act of Driscoll to his frenzied search for self. Doris Alexander notes the inspiration behind

Yank being baffled by why Jimmy killed himself by jumping overboard in mid ocean. He questions that "why Driscoll, proud of his animal superiority and in his complete harmony with his limited conception of the universe, should kill himself" (246).

Extremely expressionistic, the play strongly condemns the dehumanising effect of globalisation. Although the play is from early twentieth century, the relevance it holds even today is amazing. Globalisation has stripped off our identity as we are not who we think we are (Saravanan). Yank is the epitome of a myopic vision as he thinks his job is of paramount importance. He is content to be a stoker with a "superior strength" as compared to the other stokers (Batra; THA 76). He defends the ship as his home when he says with fierce contemptuousness, "Shut up, yuh lousey boob! Where d'yuh get dat tripe? Home? Home, hell! I'll make a home for yuh! I'll knock yuh dead. Home! T'hell wit home! Where d'yuh get dat tripe? Dis is home, see?" (Batra; THA 84). He considers his work vital. Long and Paddy, his two co-workers, try to oppose this idea but are met with a strong resistance. Long in part agrees with Yank to call the "stinking ship" his home but puts the blame on the "damned capitalist clarss" (Batra; THA 84). Paddy however, reminisces about his days on a clipper ship when men were called the sons of sea and had the freedom to sit under the starlit skies and dream. He scornfully exclaims the reality behind these streamliners, "…wid divil a sight of sun or breath of clean air- chocking our lungs wid coal dust- breaking our backs and hearts in the hell of the stokehole- feeding the bloody furnace- feeding our lives along wid the coal, I'm thinking- caged in by steel from a sight of the sky like bloody apes in the Zoo!" (Batra; THA 90). This does not break Yanks strong resolve to belong to the ship and he disdainfully tells Paddy that:

Tinkin' and dreamin', what'll that get yuh? What's tinkin' got to do wit it? We move, don't we? Speed, ain't it? Fog, dat's all you stand for. But we drive trou dat, don't we? We split dat up and smash trou- twenty-five knots a hour! (*Turns his back on PADDY scornfully.*) Aw, yuh make me sick! Yuh don't belong! (Batra ; THA 94)

Mildred is Yank's employers' daughter who is terrified by his "abysmal brutality" (Batra; THA 110). She represents the capitalist moneyed class who has a Midas touch. She is explained in the stage directions as, " …a girl of twenty, slender, delicate, with a pale, pretty face marred by a self-conscious expression of disdainful superiority. She looks fretful, nervous and discontented, bored by her own anaemia" (Batra; THA 96). Mildred is dressed in an all-white attire to "discover how the other half lives" which stands in a complete contrast to the bad lit soot covered stokehole (Batra; THA 98). The artificial Mildred who also finds herself as a "waste product in the Bessemer process" (Batra ; THA 98), is also searching her motive in life. However, she is going to the stokehole in order to get a "new thrill"(Batra ; THA 100). Mildred is as artificial and lifeless as her white dress which she would dump in the ocean once she's back from the stokehole.

Mildred makes Yank not only question his identity as a mighty stoker but also makes him realize his ugliness and his inability to look beyond the stokehole of a transatlantic liner. Before she enters the scene Yank is throwing his weight around and is quite confident of his work. He says to the engineer, "(Shaking his fist upward- contemptuously.) Take it easy dere, you! Who d'yuh tinks runnin' dis game, me or you? When I git ready, we move. Not before! When I git ready, get me!" (Batra ; THA 108). But when Mildred sees him she covers her face and calls him a "Filthy beast" (Batra; THA 110). It is this that makes Yank question himself and his role which is further aggravated by Paddy who re-enacts the scene to only make Yank doubt himself. He confirms and affirms that Yank is a Hairy Ape. Long also pitches in and the entire thing turns out to be nothing short of an insult, he says, "Hinsultin' us! Hinsultin' us, the bloody cow! And the bloody engineers! What right 'as they got to be exhibitin' us 's if we was bleedin' monkeys in a me Nerie?" (Batra ; THA 114).Yank continues to find ways to take his revenge and ultimately ends in jail and is also rejected by Industrial Workers of the World (I.W.W) where the secretary calls him a brainless ape. Unable to find his bearings he walks towards a zoo. Calling the gorilla his brother Yank draws similarities between them. The gorilla smothers him to death. This is how Yanks fatal quest to belong ends. Eugene O'Neill shows that our identities our made up of class which is already set in stone.

Mildred found Yank no less than a beast but she rocks his world upside down when she insults him "…in the very heart of his pride" (Batra; THA 110). Three weeks later Yank tries to find closure by attacking people on the Fifth Avenue in order to take his revenge if not from Mildred than from people who are like her. Instead of retaliating they bypass him. The word "Monkey fur" from a woman drives him to violence (Batra; THA134). He expresses his pent up fury by attempting to pull off the lamp pole. He is arrested by the police. When Yank finds himself in the prison, that is when reality hits him and he finds out about Industrial Workers of the World (I.W.W). After getting thrown out by Industrial Workers of the World (I.W.W) he gets lonely and purposeless. With no aim left in his meaningless life he goes to zoo to feel one with gorilla and finally ends his futile journey of belonging. Disillusioned by all these happenings he finally tries to categorise himself with the gorilla in a zoo and is smothered to death by him.

Yank and Mildred struggle with their identities and look for reasons to belong. The former represents the animalistic side and the latter shallowness. Coming from the extremes of the same spectrum both yearn to belong and are just like a leopard cannot change its spots. Yanks actions are outcome of his frustrations. Pushed to a corner, he actually reacts in a way totally unacceptable to the outside world. Yank commanded respect because of his robustness. However, he was unable to process complex cerebral issues. He would very often physically sit in the position of Rodin, The Thinker, but couldn't "tink" clearly. He found the firemen superior to all- "What's dem slobs in de foist cabin got to do wit us? We're better men dan dey are, ain't we? Sure! One of us guys could clean up de whole mob wit one mit" (Batra; THA 86). Furthermore, delving into this comparative contrast, he continues, "put one of 'em down here for one watch in de stokehole, what'd happen? Dey'd carry him off on a stretcher. Dem boids don't amount to nothin'. Dey're just baggage. Who makes dis old tub run? Ain't it us guys? Well den, we belong, don't we? We belong and dey don't. Dat's all" (86).

He made the ship his home and was extremely proud to run the stokehole. When Paddy started comparing and reminiscing about his clipper ship days he vehemently and excitedly not only defended the transatlantic liner but also stressed the importance of his role in running the huge ship. He did not undermine his position of staying at the base of the ship since he was in complete charge of moving the whole thing.

Yank loved his work and made everybody work as hard as they could. He treated the ship like a baby and would put in all his might in running it. He also pushed his co- workers to work hard and kept boosting their morale throughout, "Come on, she needs it! Give her pep! It ain't for him. Him and his whistle, dey don't belong. But we belong, see! We gotter feed de baby! Come on!" (Batra ; THA 108). He was a man of self-respect because when Mildred called him a "filthy beast" he retorted by saying "God damn yuh!"(Batra; THA 110). Yank also wanted to take revenge by outwitting her. He was utterly disgusted by Mildred's reaction and wanted to teach their class a lesson because she insulted him in his workplace where he thought he belonged. After few days he starts a rampage on the fifth avenue only to be sent to prison where he finally transitions from an ape to a thinker. He says, "Nobody gets me but me, see? I started to tell de Judge and all he says was: "Toity days to tink it over." Tink it over! Christ, dat's all I been doin' for weeks!" (Batra; THA 138).

Being directionless in his meaningless life he asks the policeman in a mocking voice about his next destination, to which the policeman curtly replies "Go to Hell" (Batra; THA 154). Finding himself with a gorilla he thinks he finally belongs, he admits that his stokehole life was a metaphorical cage and now he is completely helpless and miserable. The play's title strikes the keynote to the entire drama. It suggests that *The Hairy Ape*'s humanized form is Yank. The entire play reads like a journey expressing Yank's alienation and his futile efforts to belong in the society. The play studies disintegration of modern civilization. They are pointers to a contemporary civilization where science and technology have encroached into the territory of spirituality and has disintegrated into spiritual paucity, loneliness, isolation and a loss of values.

IDENTITY CRISIS IN DESIRE UNDER THE ELMS

It is a play of tangled, lonely personalities whose passions are thwarted by the trivial yet intense exaltation of life. All the characters' desire for ownership of a farm that ultimately led to their downfall. The brooding elms, serene cows, harsh God and self-centred exploitative characters who can go to any extent to satiate their primal lust of possessiveness and revenge make the play a timeless classic. The people's mind in this story are tangled with loneliness, thwarted passion, the trivial, the intense exaltation and denial of life. Underneath this solitude, desire works the redemption through love.

In this play children of old Ephraim Cabot hate him. The youngest son is Eben who is Ephraim Cabot's son from second wife. He remembers his dead mother and sees her around the place rising from the grave. The father brings home a third wife. The two older sons, Simeon and Peter, go away to California; Eben stays and thinks to avenge his mother. As the time passes Eben and Ephraim Cabot's third young wife Abbie come to love each other. A son is born, which old Ephraim Cabot thinks is to be heir to the farm, leaving the second wife's son, Eben, adrift in the world. While a dance in the honour of the new born child goes on in the kitchen, Ephraim Cabot and Eben quarrel outside. Eben believes Ephraim Cabot when he hears that Abbie wanted a son only to cheat Eben of his property. When Eben confronts Abbie, she kills the child in order to prove her love for Eben. Eben runs off to call the sheriff. Meanwhile, Ephraim Cabot turns the livestock loose in the woods and plans to go away. He finds the money gone from his hiding place. Eben returns from the sheriff, he falls at Abbie's knees, takes part of the blame on him, and both go away together to prison.

The play is notable for its vivid characters. Though almost all the characters have been drawn effectively, the portraits of Ephraim Cabot and of Abbie are especially important. Ephraim Cabot is a shadow patriarch as he cannot guide his sons properly. He is the synoptic centre of all vices like greed, lust, power and possession. Being a domineering personality, he makes his sons slog like animals on the farm but ultimately the passion to possess the farm turns the sons against the father thereby further straining their relationship. His ego is of monumental proportions. His name Ephraim in Hebrew means fruitful. However, his role is completely contrary to the Biblical one. He is responsible for his family's downfall. Being away from farm for more than two months he comes back home married to his third wife, Abbie. Both Simeon and Peter poke fun at him and leave the farm for better work opportunity in California. Ephraim Cabot marries Abbie not out of love or lust but out of sheer loneliness. However, he is still down in the dumps and seeks solace in the cows even after being married to Abbie. He confesses to Abbie that he will set the farm on fire before his death so that nobody can own it. This shows his fierceness to possess the farm. Indulgence in the farm and negligence of his filial responsibilities are his tragic flaws. This obsession with the farm, denunciation of pleasures and maliciousness towards his sons along with his rocky nature are nothing but projections of his repression. Ephraim Cabot cannot maintain equilibrium in reason as well as instinct and succumbs to his devilish instincts. He has not only suppressed his urges but also caged himself in the farm.

Ephraim Cabot in his fierce possessiveness burns down the farm, and everything on it, so that nobody can own the farm. He has an ego of monumental proportions. For what he really represents is pure power both physically and emotionally. Ephraim is also a prisoner of the farm over which the sinister shadow of his dead wife's motherhood broods, torturing him with a tyrannical love that makes him guilty. Doris Falk, an American author and educator, comments on this relationship saying that the father and mother have no escape from each other as they are "interlocked in a continual context for power and authority" (34). He asserts that however they appear to be the binaries of each other, yet are "immitigable archetypes into which all unicellular life must divide"; and on gender binary ground- "man in space and time must always be composite work of the two. Man, because of his very humanity, must needs be torn between the Father's love of power and the Mother's power of love" (34).

Ephraim Cabot tells in a highly revealing speech how he punished himself by a life of farming in rocky, forbidding soil, his pleasure in hard work, a masochistic denial of his repressed sexual needs. Ephraim Cabot has in him many strokes of grey shade. He is a shadow patriarch as he cannot guide or mend his sons in a proper way. The tussle for material wealth sets the father against the sons thereby transmuting the filial love into hatred. He is a domineering father and all his sons though afraid of him, later rebel one by one. His philosophy in life is toil and trouble. Ephraim Cabot is a typical hard-hearted patriarch and for O'Neill, the father figure. He boasts of his physical strength and manhood, and his Biblical name Ephraim. The play begins with the conversation between Simeon and Peter, and it is informed that their father departed from home two months ago, and nothing has been learned of him since then. It is for the first time in thirty years, ever since he married his second wife Eben's mother, that he has been away from the farm. They have not received any message from him and as he was old, naturally they think that he is dead. They do not love him for he made them work hard like slaves. Eben, who has been heeding to his half-brothers from the window, also concurs with them in wishing his father dead. He is of the opinion that his mother died of overwork as Ephraim Cabot forced her to work hard on the farm. He himself could not succour her because he was too young at the time. As he is mature now, he wishes to retaliate for the wrong done to her. He would stand up for her and affirm facts to his father. His mother's spirit is troubled and restless but he would avenge for her, so that she may rest in peace in her grave. When Eben delivers the hearsay that their father, Ephraim Cabot has married again, Simeon and Peter are determined to leave home. So, they curse their father, mock, jeer and stage a dance before him to celebrate their emancipation. Ephraim Cabot is dumb-founded at the insolence and impertinent conduct of his sons. They fling stones at Abbie and mockingly tell that they would rape her and burn the farm. Their father stands amazed, gazing at them, and curses for their undutiful departure.

The primal father-son conflict is enacted unconsciously by every generation, and this theme is predominant. This clash is ingrained in human psyche and is a universal phenomenon. Ephraim Cabot feels isolated and hence marries Abbie. Though he is old however, he doesn't accept it. Ephraim Cabot is lonely not only in the presence of his sons but also his new wife. When Abbie doubts whether Ephraim Cabot would leave the farm to Eben, Ephraim Cabot replies that in his dying hour, he would set his farm on fire, so that nobody can own his property. He laments about the looming shadow of loneliness in the farm and his going after women when solitude made him distraught. He feels Abbie is not interested in him and proceeds to the cows who he thinks will give him peace. Meanwhile, Abbie has sexual relation with Eben and bears him a son, which is unknown to Ephraim Cabot. When Eben affirms to Ephraim Cabot that the farm belonged to him, Ephraim Cabot retorts that the farm will belong to the baby who is going to be born to Abbie. The tragic flaw of Ephraim Cabot lies in his indulgence in instinctual pleasures and comforts and the concomitant negligence of his family's liability. He is unable to maintain a balance between instinct and reason. Later, his instinct begins to reign supreme over his reason thereby upsetting the glossy run of the actions in the family. Ephraim puts on a mask. He has suppressed his legitimate urges, has viewed love as lust, and has defied the puritanical creeds.

Ephraim Cabot has been glued to his farm which is a cage to him and is now condemned to stay on the farm. The amplified ego, the denunciation of sex, his wealth and cruelty to his sons and his rocky nature all are the projections of his repression. His real- self has been crushed and his own projections create difficulties for him making him an existential character. That is the reason he finds that he could attain peace of mind by going down to the barn, which is the only place of solace, and talking out his emotional disturbances with the cows, who offered an understanding ear.

Eben, is the victim of Oedipus complex intercepted between the father's appetite to possess and the mother's craving for reprisal. The incest with his stepmother is an outlet for this double accomplishment and a means of normalizing his psychic urges. The mother fixation ascertains his stimulation to the advances of Abbie. He is sexually enticed towards Abbie from the very beginning, but repulses her calls and perceives her with hostility. Ultimately, he succumbs to her seductions because he understands that this would be a suitable revenge. He senses that his consent to love Abbie has gratified his mother and her soul would henceforth repose in peace. Eugene O'Neill employs the mother archetype to probe into Eben's personality. Eben recounts to Simeon and Peter of the adoration for his mother and the repugnance for his father. He lodges a gripe against his father's demeanour to her. "Didn't he slave Maw t'death?" (Batra; DUE 84). To which Peter rejoins thus, "He's slaved himself t' death. He's slaved Sim'n' me' n' ye t'death – on'y none of us hain't died – yit" (Batra; DUE 84). For this exploitation, Ephraim Cabot is never exonerated, and Eben takes retribution on him by seizing his third wife and by rendering intense love to her. Abbie is the foremost woman with whom Eben comes into contact, and hence plays a great role in his personality development. When Ephraim Cabot informs that Abbie has been utilizing him as an instrument for begetting a son for Ephraim Cabot and for seizing away the farm of his mother, Eben goes wild. This spawns a misconstruction in the relationship between Abbie and Eben and, Abbie pleads, "He won't steal! I'd kill him first! I do love ye! I'll prove t'ye" (Batra; DUE 168). To validate this, Abbie kills her new born baby. Eben runs to sheriff to complain. Returning home and perceiving her truly repentant Eben finds that he too is guilty of insinuating her to slaughter the child. O'Neill attempts to turn this tale of adultery and infanticide into something of a modern Oedipus, where a strong passion gains a kind of glory.

In order to fathom Eben's reason for loving Abbie, it is imperative to analyse not only the story of Oedipus but also Freud's oedipal complex. In the story-myth of Oedipus, adopted by Sophocles in his *Oedipus Rex*, Oedipus unknowingly murders his father and marries his mother. This myth forms Freud's oedipal complex theory. Freud found a recurring pattern of attraction for the parent of the opposite sex and, jealousy, hatred and even a death wish towards the parent of the same sex that he eventually named the Oedipal Complex. Eben finds his father in competition, first for his own mother and then for his stepmother's love. Like Oedipus, Eben does not intentionally perpetrate his crime, but his fury and betrayal gives Abbie the stratagem of murdering their son to substantiate her love. Eben partakes in his maltreating by succumbing himself to the police and sharing the blame with Abbie for their son's murder. Though Eben is a much smaller character than Ephraim Cabot, his act of sacrifice for love is something admirable. The themes of possessiveness and revenge are unified in Eben's quest for a harmonious adult life for he is the victim of an Oedipus complex, caught between the father's desire to possess and the mother's desire for revenge. The incest with his step mother is an outlet to seek vengeance. Abbie's marriage to Ephraim Cabot is in itself the mother's first act of revenge: for she marries Ephraim for the same reason as he had married Eben's mother that is for the possession of the farm. Furthermore, the mother obtains her natural fulfilment for sex through adultery of Abbie, her symbolic incarnation. For the lover themselves, their coming together results in a self-knowledge, and a transfiguration of their initial desires. Eben's desire for revenge and Abbie's for the farm, changes concomitantly into a desire for each other. By killing her child, Abbie proves that her lust has become love; and by unconsciously sharing the crime, Eben murders the primordial father, whose symbolic surrogate the child really is.Abbie reveals the dramatist's power of characterization. She is aged thirty-five, she is pretty; she has married Ephraim Cabot for security. She will be mistress of a farm-house, not simply during Epharim Cabot's remaining years, but for the rest of her life. There is a strong determination in her. Michael Manheim described Abbie as, "She is full of vitality. Her round face is pretty, but marred by its rather gross sensuality" (24). Abbie's personality is similar to Eben's as they both share the same impatience, unsettled, untamed wild look. They are both determined and obstinate (Manheim 24). Abbie's murder of her child is her attempt to be God, but the act of self-denying will, the sin against love and life , is more proper to the services of Ephraim Cabot's God than to hers. Hearing of her action, " Eben: Oh, God A'mighty! A'mighty God! Maw, whar was ye, why didn't ye stop her? " To this, Abbie replies, "She went back t' her grave that night we fust done it, remember? I hain't felt her about since" (Batra; DUE 172). Her words suggest that perhaps now the ghost will return and wander restlessly, since the God has left. The most striking quality in Abbie's character lies in the complexity in her inner life of multiple desires. For Eben's sake, Abbie is prepared to sacrifice her child. Her complex character is suddenly resolved into Eben's ardent lover. She must give her grown up son anything he wants, even his own child's death. O'Neill sets the stage of the play with the description of elms that have an ominous and evil presence.

Eugene O'Neill's use of symbols become evident in his description, where he compares the elms to tired women who have overpowered the roof of the house. The elms are the only soft things on this rocked-ribbed farm however. Ephraim Cabot's real rival is the dead wife, demanding the restitution of an ancient wrong, unleashing the fury of her vengeful, and violated maternity. She is the elm tree described in the stage directions.

IDENTITY CRISIS IN THE GREAT GOD BROWN

The play *The Great Brown Head* is a puzzling tragedy of divided souls and dual personality. It is also a mockery of the American ideal of success and materialistic modern man. It weaves mythology with sociological and interpersonal themes. In *The Great God Brown*, Eugene O'Neill was determined to show the character's trauma and their mental anguish. The characters try to transcend their situation through pagan celebration of God Dionysius as well as individual's creativity. O'Neill's explanation that helps to understand the play better is quoted in Savithri Subramaniam's thesis:

Dion Antony - Dionyseus and St. Antony- the creative Pagan acceptance of life, fighting eternal war with masochistic life-denying spirit of Christianity as represented in St. Antony - the whole struggle existing in the modem day in mutual exhaustion - creative joy in life for life's sake frustrated, rendered abortive, distorted by morality from Pan into Satan, into Mephistopheles mocking himself alive: Christianity once heroic in martyrs for its intense faith, now pleading for intense belief in anything even in God keep itself. (Subramaniam 81-82)

Dion and Brown duality and their different personalities along with their wants and desires add to the theme of the play. Barret H Clark, historian, critic and literary giant asserts that, "The background pattern of conflicting ideas in man's soul to be mystically within and behind (the characters) giving them significance beyond themselves"(182). Tracing the genesis of this play one can notice that Eugene O'Neill's own life being projected into the play. Eugene O'Neill had a troubled and disturbed family. He is Dion of the play and his brother Jamie is Brown. In order to articulate his thoughts properly Eugene O'Neill seeks the help of myths and masks and makes them an important vehicle to probe his personal tragedy. Billy Brown represents the typical American businessman who is a complete embodiment of the great American dream which highlights that with hard work anyone can be successful. He is of the Apollonian order who is non-artistic and lacks vision. However, with the progression of the play we see him deteriorating from a businessman to any man who is misunderstood by the society he represents. His parents are nudging yet encouraging. They both have really high aspirations for their son. The father says, "Billy's got the stuff in him to win, if he'll only work hard enough" (O'Neill 13). Billy dutifully obeys his parents' wishes and ensures them that he will work hard. He tries to propose to Margaret in the starting of the play when they are nearly eighteen years old. He blurts out to her his fondness of her but she first ignores his proposal and then retorts with an amused laughter that she only likes him as a brother. After seven years Dion expresses his astonishment at Billy's bright and successful career as an Architect. Dion celebrates his own failure and is dismissive of Billy's success.

Billy loves Margaret with all his heart and soul and modestly admits to her that the reason behind his prosperity is "mostly luck" (O'Neill 34). She goes to Billy to indirectly ask for a job for Dion. Billy is very considerate and smitten by Margaret and instead makes it look like he himself is in need of a draftsman.

Later when he finds Dion, he rebukes him for his reckless behaviour and implores him to take his family's responsibility seriously. Being a good friend, he lays down his proposition of hiring Dion as he needs somebody to "lend me a hand down at the office" (O'Neill 42). After seven more years Billy is referred to as "...the ideal of the still youthful, good-looking, well-groomed, successful provincial American of forty" (O'Neill 41). Dion has been working with Billy but has found complete solace in the maternal arms of Cybel. Out of sheer curiosity Billy asks Cybel the reason that makes Dion so attractive to women, to this Cybel responds that "He's alive" (O'Neill 53)! After finding out about this he ensures that neither Cybel nor her imaginary sister entertain Dion. "At least--I'll give you anything you ask! --please promise me you won't see Dion Anthony again!" (O'Neill 53). By doing so Billy not only protects Margaret but also indirectly tries to control Dion's life. He envies Dion's life as he longs to be like Dion.

Dion impulsively heads to the bourgeois like house of Brown to question his actions and his intent. He wants to coax him to know the motive behind his actions. It was Billy's dirty bullying trick that made Dion wear the mask of Pan. Dion mocks Billy's inability to create and procreate. Dion sees Billy as a secure God of corporate materialistic society who is piled in layers of protective fat. He implores him and clarifies that Billy lacks the ability to create and has always been afraid of him and in awe of him. Dion dies after the confrontation and Billy buries him in his garden. The last words of Dion move Billy to a jealous duplication of Dion's life. Envy is the cause of Billy's downfall. Billy now wears Dion's mask and becomes an ideal husband for Margaret. He tries to reason out his lying to Margaret with Dion's mask. However, he comes to the conclusion that it wasn't Dion who died that night but Billy himself. Billy discloses his inner fears and apprehensions in another bitter conversation with Dion's mask wherein he admits to being infertile. "She will have children by me! (He seems to hear some mocking denial from the mask. He bends toward it.) What? (then with a sneer) Anyway, that doesn't matter ..." (O'Neill 75).

This makes Billy splintered into three personae i.e. Dion's evil mask, his own mask and his true self without the mask. The transformation of William A. Brown alias Billy to Dion Brown is heart-breaking as he tries to be somebody he is not and the evil despicable mask of Dion gets the worst of him. At last the police shoots him . His transformation to Dion Brown is complete and validated by Cybel whom he calls Mother and dies in her warm lap yet again yearning for Love. Billy exemplifies those who comply with the society's unattainable benchmarks and die trying to achieve it thereby burying with them the hopes and ambitions of a materialistic citizen of a great civilized nation. He is at war with himself and ultimately becomes a tortured amalgamation of the Dion and Brown. Billy is not only haunted by Mephistophelean Dion's mask, Margaret's vision of ideal male but is also tortured into bending over backwards to fit into ideal societal roles. Billy wants to live the life of Dionysian Dion. So as to gain power to live creatively Billy sells his soul which is made self-destructive by frustration. Billy's quest is completely thwarted as he loses both his materialistic happiness and the love he expects by donning Dion's mask. He is the Mammon of the materialistic society and showcases the anguish of an uncreative man. At last he realizes that faith is going to redeem him of his sins and poignantly seek God's forgiveness and love. Brown has epitomized the worldly success and glorification of wealth.

Sophus Keith Winther, Danish-American professor and novelist, in his work has underlined the play to be a scathing denunciation of the puritanical ideals. In Brown's life there is a glorification of the material success and wealth. His ideal is profit, and he has sacrificed other values of life for this. Commenting on the play, John Howard Lawson, an American screenplay writer, in "Eugene O'Neill" said that the play tends to prove that "men without will and environment are not men", and that the play is replete with the 'factual' and 'melodramatic' relationships (43). He goes on to assert that, "It takes no dual, or plural, personality to explain that Brown loves Dion's wife and wants to take his place". He further adds that there is "no "background pattern" which conforms to the author's intention; the disorganized expressions of purpose, which slip from the characters almost in spite of themselves, are all that distinguish them from lumps of clay" (43).

Brown cannot create as Travis Bogard, author and writer on O'Neill, explains, "for creation depends on vision and Brown moves in the dark" (276). Brown doesn't wear a mask in the beginning of the play. He has followed his parent's aspirations of becoming an architect. He confirms to his parents' wishes and submits unquestioningly to his father's legacy. Brown represents those societal standards which exploit as well discourage artists. He uses Dion's talents to transform his pedantic drafts into money-making business. Doris Falk confirms that Billy Brown is a creature and not a creator as he is a hollow and shallow businessman who is empty inside. He doesn't have a vision and is just a leftover product that glorifies materialistic myth of America (103). Brown is Dion's foil in the play. Dion helps in Brown's growth and adds to his development as an individual. Brown is fully aware of Dion's creative talents. Dion not only has artistic capabilities but also Margaret. Brown wants both these possessions of Dion. However, it is a big mistake. He pays a huge price for taking Dion's mask and trying impersonate him. Dion before his death gives his mask to Brown and in a way settles scores with Brown for exploiting him. Savithri concisely explains, "It is as Mephistoples Dion falls stricken at Brown's feet - as having condemned Brown to destruction by willing him his mask, but this mask falling off as he dies, it is the Satan who kisses Brown's feet in abject contrition and pleads as a little boy to tell him a prayer" (87). After taking Dion's mask Brown finds himself in a double bind. He has to hide Dion's body and also deal with Dion's Mephistophelian mask. This mask cajoles and makes him feel alive. Brown is lacking in moral security as he is guilt ridden and makes his life a living hell. The futility of this exchange is asserted by Raghavacharyulu who says "oppressed by a corrosive sense of guilt, he learns the failure of success" (64).

This tension of keeping dual identity harasses Brown. He tries to get rid of the effects that Dion's mask has had on him. However, he is charged with murdering Dion . This ultimately results in his own death as the police shoots him. Doris Falk explains in *Eugene O'Neill and The Tragic Tension* Brown's paradoxical situation as he can't get rid of Billy Brown without killing Dion Anthony (105). Savithri explicates in her thesis, "The final ironic twist is a statement of his dilemma, that he cannot kill the Billy Brown in himself without killing also its opposite, the Dion Antony, for as Cybel recognizes he is now Dion Brown" (88).

Dion represents the artistic Dionysian full of creativity but marred by the materialistic society. His name is a short form of his representative deity. His alcoholism and carousing connect him to Dionysus's divine portfolio. He is an artist figure, self- tortured by having to corrupt his Dionysian art in order to decorate Brown's functional buildings with Apollonian beauty in order to support his family. Dion is an awfully entangled character not only physically but also mentally. His erratic and esoteric nature is vividly shown by his mask. As the play moves forward the mask seems to show his divided self between the head and the heart. In the play, the "mask is a fixed forcing of his own face – dark, spiritual, poetic, passionately supersensitive, helplessly unprotected in its childlike, religious faith in life – into the expression of a mocking, reckless, defiant, gaily scoffing and sensual young Pan" however, by the second act one can see the arc of change even the real face has gone through as it has now become "that of an ascetic, a martyr, furrowed by pain and self-torture, yet lighted from within by a spiritual calm and human kindliness" while "the mask is now terribly ravaged. All of its Pan quality has changed into a diabolical Mephistophelean cruelty and irony" (O'Neill 47). This is an index of the extent to which Dion's life has sunk into frustration, decay, self-withdrawal and frustration. The slow change of mask shows his internal bitterness to the defiant and self-mocking Mephistophelean mask. The mask stifles both the real Dion and itself.

Dion adorns the mask to protect him from the mechanized utilitarian world. He fails to uphold the standards of art and beauty and wears the mask to feign conformism to the business-oriented world. He is in deep agony and questions the need of wearing the mask as an "armor" (O'Neill 20). The mask begins as an image of a Dionysian character but is corrupted by the societal pressures to provide for his family and the utterly frustrating materialistic needs of life represented by William Brown, the Great God of Success. Dion has to batter his soul away to the visionless creations of a mundane world. So instead of painting natures emanations he is made to turn to sketching buildings and structures. This annoys him to admit that the structures he sketches are lifeless, "Ha! And this cathedral is my masterpiece! It will make Brown the most eminent architect in this state of God's Country…. He only believes in the immorality of the moral belly" (O'Neill 63). Dion wants to be an architect because it "sounds less laborious". While he is standing at the casino pier he can only "seek the monkey in the moon" (O'Neill 17). Right from the beginning Billy compares himself to Dion and always finds himself lacking in his poet like qualities. He says, "I think the Rubáiyát's great stuff, don't you? I never could memorize poetry worth a darn. Dion can recite lots of Shelley's poems by heart" (O'Neill 18). The love and fondness that Margaret has for Dion can also be seen in the beginning of the play wherein Billy tries to propose but Margaret is lost in Dion's thoughts. She is completely bowled over not only by his dancing and singing but also painting and poetry. She compares him to a baby and mulls over his shyness and despondency.

Dion is imploring his need to wear a mask as his armor because the world is a cruel place where there is no value of love. But for Dion , "All the world loves a lover... Love is a word--a shameless ragged ghost of a word--begging at all doors for life at any price!" (O'Neill 22). The moment he gets to know that Margaret loves him he thinks he can finally be himself and won't be in need of his mask. He likens it to being reborn and outgrowing the brutal mask. However, when Margaret doesn't recognize him without the mask his dream of finally being understood dies a tragic death. The evil mask laughs wildly and bitterly at Dion and he, although shattered, admits to Margaret that he loves her "By proxy, I Love you" (O'Neill 25). She is not the refuge he has been anxiously seeking. Love is the great integrating power that leads to happiness but for them it's something fleeting which requires a sustained quest. After a passage of seven years Dion rarely speaks to Margaret and spends most of his time drinking and gambling. Margaret calls him her oldest child but Dion mockingly appreciates their inability to communicate and connect. He says, "This domestic diplomacy! We communicate in code-- when neither has the other's key!" (O'Neill 28). Margaret being the doting and considerate wife tricks Billy into giving Dion a job after they have spent all the money, they had from selling Dion's fathers company to Billy.

Dion finds utter solace in the arms of Cybel, a prostitute, who recognizes Dion without his mask and doesn't need her own mask in his presence. He finds her presence intensely calming, he says, "Your hand is a cool mud poultice on the sting of thought!" (O'Neill 40) and the maternal qualities in Cybel make her treat Dion as a child and she calls him "…Kid Lucifer!" (O'Neill 41). With further passage of time Dion and Cybel's friendship has grown which has made even Cybel's drab apartment fertile with his mere presence. They both discuss at length love and life where Dion confesses his unwillingness to go on living this mechanical life and want to "To fall asleep and know you'll never, never be called to get on the job of existence again" (O'Neill 49). However, Dion's mask is now diabolically Mephistophelean. Billy's job proposal comes to Dion when he has lost all hopes to live because when Billy asks him to take a walk he says, "I've given up exercise. They claim it lengthens your life" (O'Neill 42). He reluctantly takes up the job offered by Billy. He is made to make a compromise with materialistic world and end his quest for happiness. As an artist he is disgusted with sketching building plans. Not only does Dion know about Billy's artistic inability but also his jealousy of him to possess all that he has. Thinking that love can save him from this torturous predicament Dion makes a last desperate attempt to make Margaret realize how lonely he is but, it all goes down the drain as Margaret, yet again, doesn't recognize him without his mask.

Dion is at Billy's to tell him how he changed from a "sensitive, self-conscious boy" to "a proud, revengeful…Prince of Darkness" (O'Neill 62). He recalls a childhood traumatic experience that made him to don the Pan mask. He narrates the incidence from time when he was four-year-old with a deadly calm. He remembers the time when he is kicked and hit by his friend for the simple reason that he was drawing a picture in the sand and his friend was unable to. He says that he was not crying after the incident because of his friend's act but him. He laments that "I had loved and trusted him and suddenly the good God was disproved in his person and the evil and injustice of Man was born" (O'Neill 60). Thereon he remembers that while he was called a cry-baby, "so I became silent for life and designed a mask of the Bad Boy Pan in which to live and rebel against that other boy's God and protect myself from His cruelty" (60). Noticing the transformation in the other boy's behaviour he says, "that other boy, secretly he felt ashamed but he couldn't acknowledge it; so, from that day he instinctively developed into the good boy, the good friend, the good man, William Brown!" (O'Neill 60).

This forced him to wear Pan mask in self-defence. Although Billy is totally ashamed and embarrassed of his dirty trick but Dion doesn't let go of it and beseeches him further to sum up what life is and what it expects of its creatures, he says, "… I've loved, lusted, won and lost, sang and wept! I've been life's lover! I've fulfilled her will and if she's through with me now, it's only because I was too weak to dominate her in turn. It isn't enough to be her creature, you've got to create her or she requests you to destroy yourself' (O'Neill 61). Dion implores and bitingly asks Billy to either be a creature or a creator otherwise life will ignore him since he is a product of "snide neutralizing of life forces--a spineless cactus" (O'Neill 61). Ultimately, Dion dies after this frenzied confrontation and boastfully declares that Billy has always been jealous of the power he needed for love because Dion is love. Post death Dion remains a fertility symbol as he is making the garden bloom where he is buried. Apart from that at last, he becomes one with the nature and therefore the creature unites with the creator.

Dion is an artist archetype. He projects the enigma of a creative artist whose spirit is clamped in an inhospitable acquisitive world of consumerism. The play showcases the downfall of creativeness in a world where wealth has been deified and material affluence is the highest craving. He cannot survive because he thinks he can't take possession of anything be it his art, love or his drafts. Dion shows a clear perception into the dilemmas the modern man is writhing under which include inner security, isolation and alienation. Dion wages an eternal war against masochistic life denying materialism that leads to a mutual exhaustion of both Billy and Dion. Dion is sapped out from his roles of an artist, a husband and a father. These roles cripple him and also make him feel suffocated. Ann Massa an American author explicates that Dion makes life briefly bearable by wearing masks and playing different roles (179). He lives a dual life as his wife Margaret loves him only with his Pan mask and not the artist underneath it. The real Dion Anthony suffers underneath the veneer. This masks therefore serves the purpose for Dion as it acts as a shield. Dion wears it to hide his true self from the wretched world including his own wife who loves the mask and not the real Dion.But leading a dual life has its own risks and repercussions on Dion's mind. This mask he wears has pride and is inert therefore it makes Dions aggressive and has sinister abilities. It is only in his final moments that Dion realizes the wickedness of his mask and the need to reunite with the world. Travis Bogard interprets transformation in Dion's act of praying at this juncture as the act of exorcising the demoniac self and pacifying the God of creativity (274).

Margaret is the love interest of both Dion and Billy. Struggling for her love destroys both of them. In the end it is clearly visible that Margaret only loved her vision of the ideal male which was a combination of Dion's passion and Billy's materialism. Right from the beginning of the play Margaret can only see personae not people. Both the men yearn to be acknowledged by her but she yearns for the ideal male. Both of them end up reshaping themselves to her desired perfect image but only end up destroying themselves in the process. Margaret is a "… pretty and vivacious, blonde, with big romantic eyes, her figure lithe and strong, her facial expression intelligent but youthfully dreamy, especially now in the moonlight" (O'Neill 17). She is just like any other normal girl who doesn't have to act something she is not in this society and her mask is an exact copy of her face. Her mask doesn't seem to create the burden that Dion or Billy's masks does. She considers Dion as a husband, a child, and also as a father figure. Just when Dion feels he has found his soul mate who will make him "one and indivisible" (O'Neill 22), she doesn't recognize Dion without his mask. Margaret desires him in a lover's role. Virginia Floyd raises concerns that she is not like the Marguerite of the Faust legend who saved her husband but she only adds to his woes by negating his presence without his mask

(318). However, she herself is comfortable in taking off her mask in front of Dion. Dion calls her his "evening star" and "Pleiades" but she only loves the Pan like mask of Dion (O'Neill 23).

After enjoying a few years of marital bliss and peace abroad Margaret and Dion's marriage seem to be on breaking point as Dion has dissipated his inheritance and left his study of architecture. Margaret reproves him for his drinking and gambling habits that first began when he came to know that he couldn't be an artist. Dion told Brown that he had destroyed all his pictures that "he'd gotten sick of painting and completely given it up" (O'Neill 35). These domestic details show clearly that, instead of love and compassion, the marital life of Dion and Margaret is marked now by resentment, indifference and misunderstanding. Both are unable to have a conversation as Dion points out "This domestic diplomacy! We communicate in code--when neither has the other's key!" (O'Neill 28). This inability to communicate is yet another reason for their strained relationship.

Margaret is a dutiful wife who is ready to take up a job at the library in order to support her family. She never seems to lament her choice in her mate and is very forgiving as well as understanding. She is frequently perturbed with Dion but never stops caring about him. She is loyal and never lets out any marital discord publically but has a very shallow understanding of her husband. She acts as a catalyst in Dion's death. However, in Dion Brown she finds her perfect man. At the end she dances alone with Dion's mask that clearly shows that she only loves Dion's mask on Billy which is an amalgamation of heart and mind. Cybel offers protection and love to Dion. She is intended to be seen as an Earth mother figure. Her name is a homonym of the Greek title Sybil or prophet. This mother earth nature makes her too disassociated to give any solace in life. Cybel knows how her real self is markedly different from her mask and is the only character in the play that is able to make peace with her reality and realization. Dion seeks refuge in her tender maternal arms as he is constantly pushed away by Margaret who herself is on her quest to find the ideal husband. Her disassociation makes her seem philosophical. She shares a platonic relationship with him and keeps advising Dion to not to take life so seriously and to cease his quest of finding meaning. She says, "You may be important but your life's not. There's millions of it born every second. Life can cost too much even for a sucker to afford it--like everything else. And it's not sacred--only the you inside is. The rest is earth" (O'Neill 49).

Dion's meticulous attention to detail and yearning for specifics blinded him to his achievements. As Cybel says of his incompetence to win at cards, "You keep getting closer, but it knows you still want to win – a little bit – and it's wise all I care about is playing" (O'Neill 47). Dion's desire to possess, to fit into societal roles and to take control is what got the worst of him. She was living just for the sake of it without questioning or burdening herself. For her taking part was more important than winning. Dion loves to be around cybel as she has a warm maternal vibe who understands Dion's problems compassionately. He waits to be around her because it only through her that he can recover and rejuvenate himself. The play was a gratifying practice for Eugene O'Neill as he found modern man's life abounding in complexities and difficulties. He had complete faith that modern man's problem could be dealt and best portrayed by using myths. Eugene O'Neill uses the real face and mask to show the conflicts between inner character and the distortions which outer life thrusts upon them. It helps us understand the modern man's dilemma who are deeply entangled to finding out the meaning to their existence which is rendered meaningless by demonic materialistic world. One must achieve the golden middle ground between the extremes and not succumb to the dictates of materialism. This play is also an attempt to reveal triumph in man's failures against life's cryptic forces that not only shapes us but also limits our existence. These torn individuals dangle between the natural impulse and the shallow worldly expectations is perfectly showcased by the use of masks. Wearing of mask is not a choice but an action forced on individuals to find acknowledgment in the society. So, one can never find peace as they are constantly haunted by masks of others and hounded by their own self.

Eugene O'Neill's characters suffer from identity crisis, the main reason being failures and they cannot relate themselves to others as they are humiliated, thwarted, frustrated and neglected by others. Eugene O'Neill, has used mask to showcase the inner conflicts of Dion Anthony. The play throws light on the misguided souls who in order to fit into the society end up making sacrifices which cost them their lives. Eugene O'Neill through this play examines the sad plight of materialistic American society. He acknowledges that sometimes amends are not made within time and sometimes the solution doesn't lie with man but in time.

GIRISH KARNAD: QUEST FOR IDENTITY

Girish Karnad is one of the pioneers in India to have profusely made use of myths, oral folk forms and narrative techniques in his plays. In this way he has made a unique, noteworthy and one of its kind contributions to Literature of India. He is an excellent playwright who makes man and his existential crisis as the focus of his writings. Although man is free however he finds himself chained: chained to social customs, traditions and norms. This makes man find escape routes and ultimately get trapped in an aporia which ultimately leads to man being disconnected, lonely, rudderless and directionless. Man, therefore, sets out on a search for self as he feels like a stranger in his own surroundings. This frustrated man is full of despair and anguish.

Quest for identity is experiential as well as existential. Girish Karnad's characters are persistently in search of their identities. In his plays the characters are yearning to find their bearings and see their real image in the society. Their identity depends on the essence of existence which is controlled by the *Purusharthas (Dharma, Artha, Kama* and *Moksha)* of man as conceived in the Indian philosophy (Karnad 72). *Dharma* refers to the spiritual; *Artha* to political and economic power; and *Kama* to aesthetics. A persons understanding of *Purusharthas* varies based on their background, sex, station in life along with the problems faced by them. *Moksha* is a freedom from rebirths and a final liberation from worldly associations (Karnad 71). One should try to keep this goal and go beyond the three realms.

In Girish Karnad's plays, characters often grapple with complex identities and the challenges they face in reconciling different aspects of themselves. Karnad's exploration of identity crisis delves into the psychological and existential struggles individuals experience as they navigate conflicting forces within themselves and their social environments.

One of Karnad's notable works, *Tughlaq*, portrays the historical figure Muhammad bin Tughlaq, who undergoes a profound identity crisis as a ruler. Karnad delves into the complexities of political power and the burdens of leadership, as Tughlaq questions his decisions and wrestles with the conflicts between personal desires and the responsibilities of his position. The play highlights the inner turmoil faced by Tughlaq as he grapples with his identity as a ruler and the consequences of his actions (Karnad 1972).

Another play by Karnad that explores the theme of identity crisis is *Hayavadana*. The play revolves around characters who struggle with fragmented identities and the search for completeness. Karnad presents the protagonists Devadatta, Padmini, and Kapila, who face existential crises as they question their incomplete and mismatched identities. The play delves into the complexities of human nature, raising profound questions about the nature of self and the limitations of human understanding (Karnad 1977).

Nagamandala, yet another significant play by Karnad, touches upon the theme of identity crisis through the lens of gender and societal expectations. The central character, Rani, is trapped in a loveless marriage and finds solace in the world of folklore and transformations. Karnad explores the tensions between prescribed societal roles and individual desires, highlighting the struggles individuals face in reconciling their personal identities with societal expectations. The play delves into the complexities of gender identity and the longing for personal fulfilment (Karnad 1990).

Karnad's plays challenge traditional notions of identity, inviting audiences to reflect on the multifaceted nature of the self and the complex interplay between personal desires, social expectations, and cultural influences. The theme of identity crisis in Karnad's works resonates with the universal human experience, as individuals navigate the complexities of self-discovery and the search for personal authenticity.

So, a man's identity is channelized in this world. Girish Karnad's play have an predominant theme of identity quest. His debut play *Yayati* is about *The Mahabharatha* legend on responsibility. Body as a force to reckon with is recognized in Girish Karnad's first play. It became a dominant metaphor in the later plays like *Hayavadana* and *Nagamandala*. *Hayavadana* took its leitmotif from an ancient tale in Sanskrit, *Vetalapanchavimsatika* retold by Thomas Mann in *The Transposed Heads*. This deals with the dichotomy between mind and body and the complexity of using folk elements such as masks and the supernatural. In *Nagamandala*, Girish Karnad gave an intriguing interpretation to a folktale about a woman's love for a cobra that impersonates as her husband. Girsh Karnad's *Yayati* is taken from *The Mahabharat*. It deals with exquisitely crafted characters of Yayati, Pooru, Chitralekha, and Devayani who are caught up in difficult circumstances. These characters are in a constant state of flux as they are caught up in a trap of situations. Yayati wants to live to the fullest, Pooru wants to match up to his ancestor's grand actions and Chitralekha is the scape goat as well as an eye-opener in this entire situation. These characters are yearning to find their root and assert their identity. They are caught up in absurdist situations and are strangers to the society. The second play *Hayavadana* deals with two friends falling in love with the same girl, Padmini. Padmini likes the body of one and the mind of the other. The play centres upon Padmini's choices and her freedom to choose the best attributes of the two men. The men are struggling to keep up with their bodies and Padmini is doubting her choices. Therefore, the characters are deserted and alone. Third play is *Nagamandala* that deals with Rani's predicaments, trials and tribulations. Her husband doesn't love her but a shape shifting *naga* falls in love with her and impersonates as her husband. Rani evolves as a character and finally finds her bearing when she passes the chastity test.

Girish Karnad's attitude has always been to extract the best from any adverse situation. This ease while dealing with perplexing, mysterious dark human corners can be observed in his mythical subduing too. The inevitable rationality in human existence is stoically handled by Girish Karnad. His plays can be observed from the point of view of an unpredictable human existence. The nostalgia and faith in his own culture probably made it possible for Girish Karnad to return to his roots.

IDENTITY CRISIS IN *YAYATI*

Girish Karnad has manifested an old-fashioned saga of *Yayati* from *Mahabharata* with a new meaning. In the *Mahabharata,* King Yayati is cursed to old age in the prime of his life because of his wife Devyani's complaint to her father Shukracharya. Yayati tries to circumvent that misfortune by demanding that his son Pooru lend him his youth in exchange for the curse. Girish Karnad's version of *Yayati* is very contemporary and alarmingly original because he rejects the traditional glorification of son's self- sacrifice. Apart from themes like lust, jealousy, racial consciousness, ambition there is also the cognizant existence of a human being which makes Girish Karnad's *Yayati* different. *Yayati* is the most mythical of Girish Karnad's plays. The play was conceived abruptly and unpremeditated. R.K. Dhawan, Indian writer and editor, summarizes the occasion and the process of its writing in *The Critical Perspectives* as quoted in Kendre Vitthal thesis titled "The Sense of History and Tradition in the Plays of Girish Karnad in The Light of Subaltern Perspective" narrates how the play was conceived. He tells one day when Kanrad was reading *The Mahabharata* before his visit to England amidst an intense emotional turmaoil, he stumbled upon the story of 'Yayati'which later shaped his play which he wrote in Kannada. In addition, he comments on the play, "hile the subject matter was purely native and traditional, the form and structure were essentially western" (Kendre 2).

Girish Karnad's originality lies in working out the galvanization behind Yayati's ultimate assortment. In *The Mahabharata,* Yayati is able to fulfil his desire. In Girish Karnad's play, however, he apprehends the trepidation of his own life and presumes his moral liability after a sequence of figurative encounters. Girish Karnad's reading of Sartre and other existentialists helped to give a contour and worth to his play. The drama, thus, provides the opportunity to look at the confrontation that the individuals face with the fanatic and bigoted system. In the starting of the play, the Sutradhara reveals the intention behind using the ancient lore as the plot of Yayati which is further highlighted in an interview of Girish Karnad with Rajender Paul, Girish Karnad said that he was excited by the story of Yayati "exchange of ages between the father and the son, which seemed to me terribly powerful and terribly modern. At the same time, I was reading a lot of Sartre and the existentialists indulge in suddenly seemed to link up with the story of Yayati" (113).

It is an existential play that deals with the theme of responsibility. Yayati is the typical representative of the common man, who in spite of enjoying happiness from varied sources, is always discontented and is always madly running in pursuit of new contentment and gratifications. He is in a world where spiritual values have entirely been swept away. Blind pursuit of bliss has become the supreme religion in his life, which ultimately leads to existentialism. It also reflects on the condition of modern man, whose mind disturbed by many worldly and sensuous passions have turned into a veritable zoo. It is bursting with wild desires, carnal pleasures, and irresponsible exercise of power. They have forgotten the imperishable values of life.

Yayati as a king is surmised to defend and counsel his citizens but he yearns for only one deed that is the nectar to be immortal. He has innate and infinite freedom. He is a fiasco both as a father and as a father-in-law. The father must cater to instability and take care of other members in the family. He must be an inspiration to his children. However, Yayati when cursed by Shukracharya, does not know how to sort out the situation. The king by transferring his old age to his son Pooru becomes a destroyer. He even blights the life of his daughter-in-law, Chitralekha. Yayati is so obsessed with the sensual pleasures of life that he never ruminates his own death. Millions of people revel in gratification throughout their life and they have their representative in Yayati. He reveals the view that each man is what he chooses to be or makes himself. Yayati in the play is introduced through Sharmishtha. In the fracas between Devayani and Sharmishtha, the latter states that Yayati married the former only for his lust for immortality – for her father's art of *'sanjeevani'*. Devayani easily trapped by the acerbic words of Sharmishtha, rejects to concede Yayati's contention that she has been very appealing to him and therefore proposed to marry her.

Yayati is shrewd to understand Sharmishtha who is the cause of all the troubles. When Yayati asserts that he would like to converse with Sharmishtha in the chamber, Devayani refuses to leave them unassisted for which Yayati says, "I am no stranger to woman, darling" (Karnad; YAYA 16). Through these words, Yayati himself brings out the truth that he is an easy-going man with woman. The conversation between Yayati and Sharmishtha brings into light the veracity about the feud between Devayani and Sharmishtha. Yayati enquires as to why she had pushed Devayani into the well; she retorts that it was because Devayani referred to her and her caste as poor people. Comprehending that nobody in the palace likes her, Sharmishtha tries to consume poison but Yayati stops her. Later, Yayati poses a question to Sharmishtha, if she really wants to put an end to her life. Yayati is ignorant of conundrum due to the liaison between Sharmishtha and himself. When Devayani entreats Yayati to send Sharmishtha out of the palace, he remarks that he has made up his mind that Sharmishtha would be his queen and Devayani his senior queen. Yayati's enticement for the female sex transcends all social bulwarks. He shamelessly states to Devayani that Sharmishtha has enthused and restored his youth to him due to which he cannot forsake her. Devayani is unable to cope up with the situation and the stage direction focuses on her gestures: "Devayani stares after him. Then, as Swarnalatha watches horrified, she tears the marriage thread from around her neck and flings it on the floor" (Karnad; YAYA31). She asserts that she is not a Kshatriya queen to suffer and departs from the palace. During the conversation between Yayati and Pooru comes the news of Shukracharya's curse that Yayati would lose his youth and become decrepit by nightfall.

When Pooru notifies that, the curse will not have the efficacy on Yayati if a young man acquiesces to take it upon himself and offer his youth as substitute, there is a sense of confidence in Yayati. He has a delusion that his people would take up his curse , but it is shattered when Pooru declares that people are prone to take upon death rather than decrepitude. Later, Pooru himself accepts the curse and informs Sharmishtha that the reason is because he wants to add a touch of mystery in his life so that he can have the grand vision as his ancestors (Karnad; YAYA50). When the son willingly proffers himself to take the curse and grows older than his father, the son fills the role of a husband to his mother. Girish Karnad, however, does not proceed in recounting anything about this. He invents the character named Chitralekha, Pooru's wife who has a major role in Yayati's life. Yayati has substantiated patriarchy when he coerces Chitralekha into accepting the 'aged' Pooru to oblige Bharata family. When she denies, he exercises his authority as her father-in-law and as a king. Chitralekha cannot bear the reality and commits suicide, and this opens Yayati's eyes. He owns the responsibility of creating havoc in the family and restores Pooru's youth.

Girish Karnad has used Myth to uncover the ludicrousness of life with all its inherent conflicts, and to show man's perpetual tussle to achieve perfection. The playwright takes a deep insight into Yayati's character. Yayati is a true ambassador of men who, in spite of enjoying pleasures in life, still feel dissatisfied. He takes Pooru's youth and later sees the indecency of his shallow action. This makes him feel alienated and lonely. He feels catastrophic disenchantment. This incompleteness makes him question his actions. Girish Karnad's characters are portrayed as those who accept the reality and reconcile and those who fail to do so. Yayati's loss of masculinity makes him realize that he is an outsider. So as to hold on to his identity of being a robust king and to maintain his identity he asks his country-men to take up his curse. He is later shocked to find that nobody wants to sacrifice their youth for him. Sharmishtha is his voice of reason who makes him realize the impropriety of his actions as she implores him about the necessity of taking Yayati's curse. She says only a fool or a person looking for holy martyrdom would take it (Karnad; YAYA 46).

Initially, Sharmistha uses her will to wreak havoc in the palace in order to retain her *Rakshashi* identity. She says, "…we rakshasas have chosen to live in chaos, proud that it is a chaos of our own creation. And yet of course we also despise ourselves for not being lucid and rational, like you Aryas. To be thus convolute is our prerogative" (Karnad; YAYA 18). Sharmishtha retaliates frequently because she has chosen to retain a particle of herself and that is being *Rakashashi*. However, we see a change in her as she is the one who seems to be balanced among all the characters. She is the one who accepts the reality of life and reconciles. She makes Yayati accept the reality of life and move on. Nobody would want to give their identity as it justifies their existence. Without rooting oneself one can never belong. Sharmishtha is fearful of the future and repercussions of Yayati's demand. She tries to deter Pooru and says that his act is a "rank perversion" (Karnad; YAYA 50). She also reminds Pooru of his young wife Chitralekha. Chitralekha is a phenomenal character that has glimpses of a feisty woman who is vocal about her wants and ready to voice her mind. She does not want to succumb to Pooru and Yayati's decision. Chitralekha ends her life for pride, assertiveness and defiance insisting upon honour and the logic of choice she makes in her life. *Yayati* is the story of this inward struggle of a being. Chitralekha also accepts the reality and chalks out her own destiny.

Pooru wants to etch out his own journey but has the burden of following in the footsteps of his forefathers. Pooru confesses, "I had not the slightest inclination to follow in the footsteps of my illustrious forefathers...I was bored by the hermitage, embarrassedly. I wanted to run away from all that it. (Karnad ; YAYA35). Instead of enjoying the luxurious and powerful position of a king, Pooru wants to be a worm. He explains his turmoil of just asking questions and sitting peacefully by not seeking answers (Karnad; YAYA 38). Pooru wants to ask the questions because he does not want to pretend to be powerful by doing what he does not wish to do. He is not frantic for answers of his questions but he does not want to follow his ancestors recklessly. Pooru's life is perturbed because he wants to search answers to questions that can help him find the purpose of his life. He does not want to follow his ancestors insensitively. The rituals cunningly performed are shunned by him. The ambiguity enlivens him but there is disintegration between the mind, that wishes and the world, which disheartens.

Yet, Pooru tries to fulfil his wish of sailing against the wind by accepting the old age of his father. But Yayati, after Chitralekha's death, realizes transient life and gives back Pooru's youth to him. And Pooru asks the question at the end, "What does it all mean, O God? What does it mean?"(Karnad; YAYA 69). Sutradhara concludes, "Pooru at last found the courage to ask a question. But was it really a meaningful question or was it a cry of despair that he could hope for no meaning?" (Karnad; YAYA 70). Pooru chooses to give away his youth for Yayati because he wants Yayati to realize his obligation. He is a choice and for him, to be is to choose himself. Later, when he accepts his young age again, he is a perfect muddled self of *Rakshasa* and *Aryas*, that is to say, egotism and altruism. B. Yadava Raju highlights the fact that Yayati was way ahead of its time and highlighted the issues of class and gender by sensitising about the subliminal tensions of the drama. He says Girish Karnad was way ahead of his times in addressing these matters in post-independence India as early as 1961 (80).

IDENTITY CRISIS IN *HAYAVADANA*

Girish Karnad's play *Hayavadana* deals with the theme of incompleteness. *Hayavadana* means a man with a horse's head. This play opens with Hayavadana trying to get rid of his absurd head. He is born to a princess who married a stallion. Hayavadana stumbles upon a stage where a play about transposed heads is to be performed. The play's Bhagavata tells him of the same *Kali* temple where play's Padmini found her solution. Bhagavata then starts to narrate Padmini's story. The plays centres on a love triangle among Devadatta, Kapila and Padmini. Padmini marries the intellectual Devadatta but is drawn towards Kapila for his well-built physique. All three of them travel to Ujjain fair and on the way come across a *Kali* temple. There the men of the play behead themselves. Padmini is blessed by Goddess *Kali* to bring back the dead to life. Padmini impulsively attaches Devadatta's head to Kapila's body and vice versa. Padmini enjoys a happy marital life as she has the best attributes of both the men because she takes the man with Devadatta's head and Kapila's body to be her husband.

After some time, it is revealed that since the head is supreme so both man's bodies change their attributes according to their heads. This is witnessed and informed to the readers by dolls which were bought from a fair. Padmini gives birth to a son but starts dreaming about Kapila's body. In the end all three find their solution in death as both men die in duel and Padmini performs *Sati*. Their silent son is given to Bhagvata. Hayavadana's wish is also granted by goddess *Kali* as he finally turns into a horse. On seeing a horse talk as humans Padmini's mute son also begins to speak and the play comes to an end. The dilemmatic yet eternal human desire for completeness and resulting existential predicaments are reconnoitred in the drama. The characters in the drama are in search of their identity which is hard to find because of their persistent and at times unreasoned desires. Human beings are bound to feel absurd because of these human desires and of the unreasonable silence of the world against it. The enticing, inherent freedom and the insurmountable change in human life make him feel the absurdity behind various situations. U.R. Anantha Murthy in his introductory note to *Hayavadana* says, "The play exposes the audience to a significant theme like 'incompleteness' in a comic mode... the play tries to create an illusion in us that the hate determines the being of man." (Murthy ii).

There is a peculiar disparity between whatever is hoped and whatever is endured by Padmini, Kapila and Devadatta. In the beginning of the play, Lord *Ganesha* is described as an embodiment of imperfection, of incompleteness, yet he is believed to be the master of success and perfection. Hayavadana, his mother, Padmini, Kapila or Devadatta are not ready to accept the decree of nature and try to achieve what their hearts desire. Girish Karnad has uses Myths to represent this incongruous skirmish. Goddess *Kali* is portrayed ludicrously. She is sleepy and easy to please which wittily exhibits the perfunctory and rigid belief in God especially in Indian context. Man craves to rebel against time, struggles to feel like home in the world, and expects confidence in humanity; but he comes to know his transience, his seclusion, his mechanical stringency. Bhagavata reveals, "Each to his own fate. Each one to his own desire. Each one to his own lack." (Karnad; HAYA 92).

The inquisitiveness of unravelling the mystery of unpredictable future is inbuilt in human nature. Padmini, Kapila and Devadatta are troubled confronting the change after the heads get transposed. Padmini is exasperated because of the cycle of change as it takes away whatever she has achieved and leaves her in ambiguous situation often. Kapila and Devadatta have to fight of the drama, both of them forgive each other and are ready for withdrawal or to sacrifice themselves because they apprehend the mad and endless dance of incompleteness. Padmini too at the end performs *Sati* for the two men rebelling against this imperfection of life. Thus, deaths highlight the absurdity of the human situation in the drama. The way, Hayavadana and Padmini struggle consistently till the end, exhibits the incongruous concepts of hope and faith. Padmini asks Bhagavata to raise her child in woods as well as in town to give him a complete life. Hayavadana goes to Goddess *Kali* and asks her to complete him, but Goddess is irritated with the act of chopping off the heads. Thus, she blesses him to be complete. He is transformed into a complete animal because Goddess *Kali* doesn't have the patience to listen to his complete prayer of transforming himself in a complete human being. This preposterous situation is suggestive of mythical concept of faith. The enigmatic change of the sadness of boy into a smile and Hayavadana becoming a complete horse in each other's company shows Girish Karnad's genius writing skills.

Devadatta is a failed poet who suffers because of his wife and friend. He is a passionate lover of beauty. In twenty years of life, he has been in and out of love fifteen times. The libido of Padmini enchants him that he fails to judge her, but Kapila easily makes out that she is too fast for the delicate Devadatta. She needs a strong man, but Devadatta cannot judge this basic difference, which results in his tragedy. Though a man of high intelligence, he perceives only the pristine beauty but fails to fathom the woman in her. The adversary of the marital joys of Devadatta is none other than his own friend Kapila. Intruding in Devadatta's personal matters, Kapila steals away the joys of married life, and very soon, he becomes the source of his agony. Kapila is Devadatta's friend but faces an existential crisis as Padmini likes Kapila. This makes Devadatta feel lonely and distant from both Padmini as well as Devadatta. He knows that there is a hidden bond between Padmini and Kapila, but dares not to question it. Devadatta loved Kapila as much as he did Padmini, but at the same time cannot endure to live with the notion of sharing his wife with anyone.

Unable to keep up the tension and anguish of isolation, he resolves to end his life, and actually does so but the fate rules otherwise. He comes to life by the intervention of Goddess *Kali*, but with the body of Kapila. It leads to a discrepancy between the will and the mask that make the poet turn away from poetry. Kapila and Devadatta yearn to be each other. Kapila longs to be Devadatta so that he can express his love to Padmini while Devadatta craves to be Kapila so that he can charm his wife and win her love. In case of Kapila and Devadatta, their conflict of identity cannot be easily resolved, and the only feasible solution to the situation is their death. There is no other way in which they could have accepted a resolution for their catastrophe, as going back to their old bodies could only have made it more intricate. After undergoing, a short interval of merriment and good days with his wife Devadatta once again loses his wife to Kapila, and his end is disastrous. He departs to the jungle where his wife had gone to meet Kapila with a decisiveness to end the love triangle. In fact, he loves Padmini too much; that is why he snubs the proposal of Kapila to live like Pandavas and Draupadi. He cannot contemplate sharing her, and so exhorts Kapila to fight a duel.

The identity crises reach its peak when Devadatta asks Kapila whether he loves Padmini, and the latter replies in the affirmative. He is a victim and scapegoat. Kapila is the perfect example of a "man more sinned against sinning" (Shakespeare). That is he tries to victimize others but in turn gets victimized. Kapila, the bosom friend of Devadatta, is dark and plain to look at, and in deeds, that require physical strength and skills, none can rival him. He possesses a strong body with rippling muscles. Girish Karnad sketches him as a rustic young man with little intelligence. With his innocence of a child, he becomes an exact opposite of the scholar Devadatta beating the latter with his greater reservoir of vitality and energy. The athlete in Kapila embodies the ultimate expression of the strength of human spirit as represented in the power and magnificence of human body. It is to this body that Padmini is allured to. Though he is friendly to Devadatta but is a shadow companion or a frenemy. When he catches sight of Devadatta dead in the *Kali* temple, like a coward, Kapila beheads himself being afraid that he would be censured. Despite their difference of physique and mind, they are characterized as *Lava* and *Kusha, Rama* and *Lakshmana,* and *Krishna* and *Balarama.* Being a true friend of Devadatta, Kapila has been always desirous of bringing joy to him. Devadatta has an immense faith in Kapila, as it is to him that he confides his cryptic. He sends Kapila on the important mission of proposing to Padmini on his behalf, though he regrets it later. Kapila executes his duty well, and wins the hand of Padmini for Devadatta. He fathoms that Padmini is not the right choice, as she needs a "man of steel" (Karnad; HAYA 90). Yet he paints Devadatta as a perfect human being due which Padmini agrees to be his wife. The personality of Kapila is altered by the presence of Padmini. The man of muscles gets enthralled by her beauty, and always hops around her. It is only she who makes him blush which he has never done before. When Ujjain trip gets cancelled, he is overcome by a strange void.

Kapila is fatally gripped in Padmini's charm. Her charisma reduces him to a puppet, and Padmini too cannot resist his vigour and starts drifting towards him. If Kapila only blushes on seeing Padmini in the beginning after the transposition of heads, he becomes more assertive and aggressive. He asserts, "I mean, you are Devadatta's wife. I have Devadatta's body now. So you have to be my wife ..." (Karnad; HAYA106). Kapila's sincerity towards Devadatta becomes his weakness. He does not like to harass Devadatta. He is so fond of him that even his love for Padmini remains a concealed reality for a long time. Though Kapila leaves for the jungle as a defeated man, he finishes up as a winner, and fares better than Devadatta. When Padmini tries to break the social barriers and meets Kapila in the jungle, he tries to persuade her to go back. Kapila tries to forget the past but Padmini's arrival makes him reminiscence.

In *Hayavadana*, Girish Karnad tries to highlight the bizarre norms of society. He also reinterpreted the folk tale to bring to light the absurdities in social behaviour. Albert Camus, French philosopher, writer and journalist, concludes:

If this myth is tragic, that is because its hero is conscious . . . Sisyphus, proletarian of the gods, powerless and rebellious, knows the whole extent of his misery: this is what he thinks of during his descent. The clairvoyance that was meant to be his torture crowns at the same time his victory. There is no fate that cannot be surmounted by scorn. (122)

To be powerless and yet have the ability to rebel is a distinctive trait of humans and of situations around oneself. This consciousness or perceptive difference does not allow one to submit to fate or to any disparaging situation. In the play, this exultant attitude for the desire to be complete is fabulously articulated by the insolent characters. The perception of the playwright is revealed by the Bhagavata that the struggle between the unfathomable nature and human desire for completeness is difficult to comprehend. Naik has rightly commented that Mann's aim was to stress the ironic impossibility of uniting perfectly the spirit and the flesh in human life while Girish Karnad tries to pose the metaphysical anguish of the human beings (137).

IDENTITY CRISIS IN *NAGAMANDALA*

Girish Karnad's *Nagamandala* is a play based on the Indian myth of shape shifting snakes i.e. *nagas*. In the play, Rani's husband, Appanna is an insensitive, unloving and carefree man who makes Rani implore for her identity in a loveless marriage. This unhappy matrimony is devoid of any physical and emotional love. Rani is a perfect picture of an unhappy exploited and troubled wife who is forced to set out on a quest of self. Rani is bound by tradition and makes up the ideal woman who follows the husband's orders unquestioningly. Adding to the importance of identity and the characters quest for it B.T. Seetha comments " if in Nagamandala the motivation is a desire to live , in Hayavadana it is a desire to become complete" (193).

Rani's story is told by a female character named story. She is deeply loved by her parents and dreams of enjoying marital bliss but her dreams are short-lived since Appanna turns out to be a bad husband. Rani is inept in adjusting to the new married life as she is unable to develop any relationship with her husband. All Indian girls are taught to be ideal wives, dutiful daughters and daughters-in-law as well as loving mothers. These touchstones establish the character of a woman in the society. Appanna represents any man who exploits and tortures his wife. He himself commits adultery and expects his wife to remain chaste. He treats her as a maid and keeps her confined to the four walls of the house as he locks the house before leaving every day to see his concubine. Rani now leads a completely solitary life away from the society. She craves to belong but is left to discover herself in her confinement. Kakar asserts that the "dominant psycho-social realities of a woman's life can be condensed into three stages. First, she is a daughter to her parents; second, she is a wife to her husband (and daughter-in-law to his parents); and third, she is a mother to her sons (and daughters)." (57). A woman establishes her identity through these three relationships.

Appanna drives Rani completely crazy and now her dreams start haunting her. Kurudava, who is Appanna's mother's friend, plays an important role in Rani's quest for identity. She gives her three different sized magical roots to entice Appanna into loving her. She says, "… Take this smaller piece. That should do for a pretty jasmine like you. Take it! Grind it into a nice paste and feed it to your husband. And watch the results. Once he smells you he won't go sniffing after that bitch. He will make you a wife instantly" (Karnad ; NAGA 34). However, when she makes the concoction of the root it turns red and her conscience doesn't allow her to feed it to her husband. The fear of getting Appanna sick with the concoction doesn't let her feed it to him. So, she throws it on to an anthill which is home to a *naga*. This shape shifting *naga* takes the form of Appanna, and falls in love with Rani. He visits her at night and they now enjoy complete wedded bliss as he loves and cares for her.

Nagamandala symbolises procreation and libido. *Naga* understands Rani's pain of being in a loveless marriage. He knew that Rani won't love any other man apart from her husband so, he tactfully wins Rani's love by impersonating as her husband Appanna. Rani throughout didn't know that the *naga* was impersonating her husband and was knowingly oblivious to the fact that the same person that is Appanna had two sides to his character. The *naga* would come to meet her during the night when Appanna was away and Appanna would return during the day just to have lunch. *Naga* flatters Rani and takes care of her. However, this happiness is short-lived as Rani becomes pregnant and Appanna doubts her chastity. This serves as a turning point in Rani's life and instead of getting subjugated she speaks for herself and retaliates boldly to Appanna's charges of adultery. She says, "Yes, there is. Give me poison instead. Kill me right here. At least I'll be spared the humiliation. Won't the cobra bite me the moment I touch it? I'll lie like your dog and your mongoose." (Karnad; NAGA 53).

This newfound courage and confidence makes Rani undergo the snake ordeal in front of the village elders. So, she vows, "Yes, my husband and this king cobra. Except for these two I have not touched any one of the male sex. Nor have I allowed any other male to touch me. If I lie, let the cobra bite me" (Karnad; NAGA58). Rani passes the test and entire village places her on a pedestal by worshipping her. The Sutradhar of the play sums up Rani's new life ," So Rani got everything she wished for, a devoted husband, a happy life. She even got a life-long servant to draw water for her house." (Karnad; NAGA59). But Appanna's qualms are not effaced and he is left thinking, "What am to do? Is the whole world against me? Have I sinned so much that even Nature should laugh at me? I know I haven't slept with my wife" (Karnad; NAGA60). Appanna is unfair to both Rani as well as his concubine. Calling Padmini and Rani to be élan vital Moutoushi Chakravartee comments that both the plays carry the burden of identity question. She states that Padmini and Rani are on the voyage of self-discovery, though unaware whether they are conscious of the fact or not. However, she postulates that the dramatist remains 'pre/occupied' with this question for tying it up with the "idea of completeness . . . Hayavadana seems completeness ... This incompleteness is a human predicament, sometimes carrying tragic consequences, which modern man has resized too well (184).

Naga saves Rani from Appanna's tyrannies and goes out of her life when he has given Rani that she deserves. *Naga* is glorified by Girish Karnad as he wants to show that a loving animal is any day better than a tyrant. However, even *naga* is rewarded by the society because when he is killed by Appanna, he is given the honour of father as Rani insists that her son perform his last rights and also yearly rituals so as to commemorate his death. *Naga* again reincarnates itself and now finds a safe haven in Rani's long tresses. Thus, silent, subdued and suppressed Rani finds her happiness and herself.

Eugene O'Neill and Girish Karnad are masters of impeccable writing and use commendable techniques to transport their readers as well as the spectators to another world. Human relations in their plays are invariably discordant. They make their characters beg for love but seldom do they experience it in a satisfying way. The characters set out on an eternal quest wherein the predicaments are perennial and the fight against them never ending. For most of the characters' death is the only way to bury the problem.

III
SUBALTERNITY IN THE SELECTED WORKS OF EUGENE O'NEILL AND GIRISH KARNAD

Literature reflects the social, cultural and economic events of an age. Through its different genres it registers and catalogues the ideas, feelings and emotions of innumerable segments of the society. The spectrum of genres it uses is vast as it could be poetry, novel, drama etc. The role of literature has transformed from its traditional didactic or pleasure principles to now reflecting the neglected as well celebrated reality of life. Literature is no longer read for delight, pleasure and aesthetics. It now works as a socio-cultural document that captures not only the liminal spaces but also otherwise ignored and neglected nuances of a society. Loomba iterates the same thought in the work *Colonialism and Postcolonialism*, "Literary texts don't simply reflect dominant ideologies but encode the tensions, complexities, and nuances within the colonial culture. Literature is a place where 'transculturation' takes place in all its complexity" (69).

In order to glorify and eulogize one thing, the other has to be condemned and denounced. This has given rise to binary opposites such as black and white, east and west, master and servant, high class and low class, etc. These opposites have resulted in dissent all over the world and given rise to two broad categories of people in the society. The first being the upper class who enjoys socio-economic privileges, authority and benefits. The second being the lower class who are socio-economically backward, dominated by others and neglected by the society. The literature of a society usually promotes and celebrates the upper class and narrates the incidents as well events from their point of view. This leads to a distortion of facts and misrepresentation of ideas by the ones registering it. In order to voice the voiceless, the historians have tried to write down literature from the lower class or marginal point of view. This initiative of rewriting history and placing the center on the margins is termed as subaltern studies.

The concept of subalternity has emerged as a critical lens through which scholars examine the experiences of marginalized individuals or groups in society. In the works of playwrights Girish Karnad and Eugene O'Neill, the theme of subalternity is explored, shedding light on the struggles, power dynamics, and social hierarchies faced by marginalized characters within their respective cultural contexts. This essay aims to provide an extensive analysis of subalternity in the works of Karnad and O'Neill, highlighting the similarities and differences in their portrayals.

Girish Karnad, an eminent Indian playwright, skilfully incorporates the theme of subalternity in his plays by giving voice to marginalized characters and delving into their experiences. Karnad explores the intersections of caste, gender, and social class, presenting subaltern individuals who challenge dominant norms and strive for self-realization.

One of Karnad's notable plays, *Yayati*, delves into the story of King Yayati from *The Mahabharata*, focusing on the subaltern characters of Sharmishtha and Devayani. Sharmishtha, a tribal princess, represents a marginalized figure navigating her identity within a hierarchical society. Karnad portrays her struggles in negotiating power dynamics, confronting caste discrimination, and seeking agency. Another significant play by Karnad, *Tughlaq,* presents the historical figure of Muhammad bin Tughlaq and his quest to establish an ideal kingdom. Within this play, characters like Aziz and Kabir embody the subaltern experience during a period of political turmoil. They challenge oppressive systems of power and reflect the subaltern's resistance against hegemonic structures.

Eugene O'Neill, a renowned American playwright, also explores the theme of subalternity in his plays, particularly through characters existing on the fringes of society. O'Neill's works depict the struggles, disillusionment, and the quest for identity among those who are socially and economically disadvantaged. In *The Hairy Ape*, O'Neill delves into the alienation and social exclusion experienced by Yank, a working-class labourer who feels disconnected from the world around him. Yank's search for belonging and identity highlights the subaltern experience. O'Neill underscores the dehumanization of the working class and emphasizes the power dynamics that perpetuate their subaltern position.

The Emperor Jones presents the character of Brutus Jones, an African-American man who rises to power on a Caribbean island. However, Jones' reign becomes a manifestation of his internalized racism and fear of the subaltern "other." O'Neill explores the consequences of oppressive systems and the struggles faced by those attempting to transcend their subaltern status.

Despite belonging to different cultural contexts, the works of Karnad and O'Neill share common themes concerning subalternity. Both playwrights delve into the psychological, social, and political dimensions of subaltern experiences, shedding light on the challenges faced by marginalized individuals. An important aspect is the intersectionality of identity markers such as caste, gender, race, and class. Both Karnad and O'Neill's works portray characters embodying multiple subaltern identities, allowing for a nuanced exploration of the challenges faced by individuals at the intersections of various marginalized positions.

Additionally, both playwrights highlight the agency and resistance of subaltern characters who strive to assert their individuality and challenge oppressive structures. They depict the resilience and determination of marginalized individuals as they navigate complex social dynamics and seek to transcend their subaltern status. The works of Girish Karnad and Eugene O'Neill offer profound insights into the theme of subalternity, portraying marginalized

The word 'subaltern' originates from an Italian word that means 'of inferior rank'. Earlier, it used to refer to army officers who were junior and were supposed to obey the orders of senior officers. Lately, this term has been used in multiple contexts. Antonio Gramsci, Italian Marxist thinker, used it in a non-military sense. The *Encyclopedia of Postcolonial Studies* explicates that Gramsci used the term 'Subaltern' in *Prison Notebooks* as a code so as to deceive the prison censor to allow his manuscripts out of the prison. Subaltern here euphemistically stands for the proletariat or working class (Hawley 425). Gramsci popularized the usage of the term in study of socio-economic theories and related concepts. He used the term in a wider context so as to include not only socio-economic and political arenas but also to denote those group of people who were non-hegemonic and socially unrecognized like the peasants, subordinate class of people or groups, non-capitalist group of people etc. These groups or classes of people are those who do not have a say and are never included in the decision-making process. Gramsci uses the term broadly in his *Prison Notebooks* to denote working class, peasants, mill workers etc. Kendre Vitthal in the thesis titled "The Sense of History and Tradition in the Plays of Girish Karnad in The Light of Subaltern Perspective" enumerates Gramsci's criteria for Subalterns as:

1. the objective formation of the subaltern class through the developments and changes that took place in the economic sphere; the extent of their diffusion; and their descent from other classes that preceded them;

2. their passive or active adherence to the dominant political formations; that is, their efforts to influence the programs of these formations with demands of their own;

3. the birth of new parties of the ruling class to maintain control of the subaltern classes;

4. the formations of the subaltern classes themselves, formations of a limited and partial character;

5. the political formations that assert the autonomy of the subaltern classes, but within the old framework;

6. the political formations that assert complete autonomy, etc. (Kendre 25)

Louai in one of the seminal works retraces the concept of subalterns and forms a timeline of evolution of the concept from Gramsci to Spivak. He states that Gramsci used the term for those who were oppressed and discriminated by the leader of the National Fascist party Benito Mussolini and his agents (6). *Post-Colonial Studies: The Key Concepts* defines the term subaltern as "sections of the people or communities who are under the command of the ruling class and subject to the hegemony of the dominant groups. It also indicates a group of the people who are denied access to hegemonic power". explaining further, "Antonio Gramsci was keen in the historiography of the subaltern classes as the history of the ruling classes is realized in the state, history being the history of states and dominant groups" (215).

Today, subaltern studies by questioning the available historical documents have produced an enormous impression on other disciplines as well. It has advocated for rewriting of history to unravel facts pertaining to the contributions made by the common people in the development of the society. In the 1980s' a project for subaltern studies was initiated under the leadership of Ranajit Guha. It claimed that the history of Indian Independence movements should be rewritten. Ranajit Guha is the most significant subaltern historian. Not only is he the founder but also the editor of subaltern studies. The subaltern historians aim to write the history from below which focuses on the lower classes or groups of the society and not the privileged elite class. Padmini Mongia in the introduction of her book, *Contemporary Postcolonial Theory: A Reader* has said that:

The idea is to write into the history of modernity the ambivalences, contradictions, the use of force, and the tragedies and the ironies that attend it. That the rhetoric and the claims of (bourgeois) equality, of citizens' rights, of self – determination through a sovereign nation state have in many circumstances empowered marginal social groups in their struggles is undeniable – this recognition is indispensable to the project of Subaltern Studies. (242)

Subaltern studies expanded its traditional boundaries and started to spread its wings to make it to other disciplines. The Preface of *Subaltern*

Studies X: Writings on South Asian History and Society explores that the book showed not only thematic concerns in subaltern studies of South Asia, but also to conduct inquiries into subalternity beyond conventional margins. They were able to perceive the effect of subalternity in the areas such as state policies, academic disciplines, literary texts, and archival sources language (Bhadra v).

Subalterns are those subjugated class of people who are economically, socio- politically and physically sidelined from main authority and power structure. Nayar highlights the importance of mapping subaltern concerns and states that these studies should focus on marginalized sections of the society and should have works written from local viewpoint and their perspectives (51). David Ludden also comments on the inclusivity of subaltern studies' growing diversity of research which now coheres like new cultural history (20). Gyan Prakash in "Subaltern Studies as Postcolonial Criticism" elucidates the impact created by subaltern studies in various disciplines and its growth as one of the significant critical studies elsewhere. "The term 'subaltern' now appears with growing frequency in studies on Africa, Latin America, and Europe, and subaltern's analysis has become a recognizable mode of critical scholarship in history, literature, and anthropology" (1476).

Literature becomes highly influenced by subaltern studies which inspired writers to make use of it to make the marginalized heard through their works and give voice to the subjugated and ignored sections of society. They wanted to get rid of racial and gender stereotypes like portrayal of low-class girls as being dumb and slow, black coloured people being animal like or drug peddlers etc. These works became vantage points for the neglected sections of the society. However, the scenario has changed leaps and bounds and the marginalized, be it based on gender, class or culture, have various avenues to vent out their frustrations and get heard.

EUGENE O'NEILL: SUBALTERN CONCERNS

Eugene O' Neill and Girish Karnad's dramatic themes focus on an individual's existential concerns in the modern society. Two important parameters that modify an individual's existential space are gender and culture. The class divides the people into categories and labels them. Gender division ensures that there is sharp divide and those females who come from lower category are doubly marginalized as they are not only poor but also from a lower category. This double bind is the outcome of a biased society and culture. Subclasses are made within a class and culture has a major role to play in this bifurcation. Dramas of Eugene O' Neill served as springboard for such ideas as he ensured this by empowering his female characters and making his male characters yearn for more than the class defined roles. His selected three plays *The Hairy Ape*, *Desire Under Elms* and *The Great God Brown* are deeply rooted in class divide and gender discrimination. Eugene O'Neill focuses on human predicaments and tries to explain the maze that leads to understanding the parameters that govern a human being's destiny. He tries to explain the ambivalent parameters that decide man's supremacy.

SUBALTERNITY IN *THE HAIRY APE*

The Hairy Ape being a multifaceted play thematically, the play presents "... a severe indictment of the modern civilization which has nothing fairer to show than a world of alienation and despair, of stratification and regimentation, of anomaly and disvalues, of lonely crowds and naked societies" (Goyal 181). The play paints a dismal picture of the working class. It highlights the horrible dehumanization, that is a result of excessive exploitation and insatiable greed along with man's everlasting quest to belong. This grim play is subtitled "A Comedy of Ancient and Modern Life" that highlights the fact that man's struggle is continuous irrespective of the time.

The Hairy Ape revolves around the subaltern coal stoker, Yank, who fights the class discrimination to assert his identity via suicide in a class dominated society that subjugates and insanely drive those at the far end of the vile social hierarchy to acts of unbridled madness and self-doubt. The stark classes divide between Yank and Mildred can be finely observed. Yank is just not an alienated have-not, but represents the human race that is as Wordsworth says "out of tune" in an impersonal mechanical world. The stokers are not only symbolically subjugated but also literally since they work in the bowels of the transatlantic ship i.e., their subjugation is two-fold.

The play is set in an enormous socio-cultural reality. Doris Alexander affirms that the play showcases a pessimistic view of industrialized America where the working class show the ape like quality and the rich are dehumanized puppets of the mechanized world (390). Eugene O'Neill's catalyst for Yank's questioning of and awakening to his true condition is Mildred who is both a destroyer and nemesis of man. It is his encounter with Mildred, who emerges out of darkness like the unconscious, shadowed side of him that rouses this slumbering automaton from slumber. Her rejection of his physical presence, the sum total of the self he had known until then, stuns him.

Yank is thrown off balance when Mildred classifies him as an animal, and his pursuit of her becomes a quest for his own identity. It reveals the class-consciousness and the handling of working class as animals. Yank takes extreme pride in his job of being a stoker in an ocean liner. He thinks he is the one that moves the world. He and the fireman is cramped up in the hot forecastle of the stokehole which is no less than a cage. The formidable description of the cage and its inhabitants show the Neanderthal Man at work.

(Batra; THA 76). Yank symbolises those who cannot find their bearings in this modern world. He showcases a type rather than an individual. Yank's nemesis is Mildred who along with her aunt are housed on the ship's best part, which is the promenade deck, where freedom, sunlight and air abounds. "…the sea all about-sunshine on the deck in a great flood, the fresh sea wind blowing across it" (Batra; THA 96). Her white dress shrieks class divide as it in complete contrast to the coal-dusted men of the stock hole. The play apart from bringing out class differences also brings out Mildred's survival in a male dominated society. Although she faints at the sight of a brute looking Yank however, she is making an effort to connect to the lower class. She is a privileged woman of early twentieth century.

Both Yank and Mildred come from different section of the society and their placement on the ship reaffirms it. Yank is very well respected and a strong leader of the stokers. Declaring his importance, Yank calls out to his mate Long, saying "run de whole woiks" over "all de rich guys dattinkdey' resomep'n, day ain't nothing! Dey don't belong, de whole ting is us" (Batra; THA 92). Mildred is a young vivacious rich girl who wants to explore the ship. When she enters the stokehole, which looks like a modern inferno, she gets a sinister vibe after seeing the bare chest gorilla like men: "A line of men stripped to the waist, is before the furnace doors. They bend over, looking neither to right nor left, handling their shovels as if they were part of their bodies ... (Batra; THA 106). Depicting their horror more vividly it says, "a flood of terrific light and heat powerful upon the men who are outlined in silhouette in the crouching, inhuman attitude of chained gorillas" (106).

For a sturdy and physically stout person like Yank thought is an exercise where he just can't make sense of the world around him. This for him was useless activity. However, thoughts or thinking becomes absolutely necessary for Yank after meeting Mildred. He feels a certain class divide which can't be overcome by physical might and now he is forced to "tink" and is hurt when his shipmates make joke of his thinking. However, shattering Yank's confidence, Mildred calls him a filthy beast. He falls from the position of leader who thinks, "de whole ting is us" to the extremity of being called a great hairy ape (Batra; THA 92). Adding insult to his misery are his shipmates who keep taunting him about being called an ape. This makes Yank set out on a quest to place himself in the society.

Yank now along with Paddy want to teach the likes of Mildred a lesson and provoke people to notice and fight with him on the Fifth Avenue. However, police first thrashes and then arrests him. The subaltern in Yank is looking for answers but he is snubbed wherever he goes. To make himself heard Yank registers with Industrial workers of the World (I.W.W), an organisation opposed to big businesses but looking at his aggressive side where he says that he will "blow up tings" and "turn tings round", they also reject him (Batra; THA 144). Inciting the organisations suspicion, Yank is thrown out and called a "brainless ape" (Batra; THA 152). Dejected and frustrated Yank goes to the zoo and finds that his plight resembles that of an ape as they are "members of de same club – de hairy Apes." (Batra; THA 156). Yank dies in the hands of the ape and as has been suggested by stage directions that finally this lost subaltern belongs, it says, "And, perhaps, the Hairy Ape at last belongs" (Batra; THA 160).

The play thus shows Yank's regression from a Neanderthal to an ape and represents the rejection, subordination, a feeling of inferiority and dissatisfaction of the working class in contrast to the mechanical but luxurious life of elite.

SUBALTERNITY IN DESIRE UNDER THE ELMS

In Eugene O'Neill's play the male characters objectify and mistreat female characters by demeaning them as well as their importance. This sexist attitude is prevalent throughout the play. The play is bursting with instances of labor power relations and gender inequality as Ephraim Cabot's rapaciousness turns the farm into an oppressive device to serve his own interests. The farm becomes a site of oppression and masculine malice where Ephraim is an unchallenged oppressor but the females thwart egomaniacal Ephraim Cabot's plan and have their presence felt throughout the play.

Ephraim Cabot made his second wife work on the farm and as per Eben she died of the grueling labor. Right from the beginning one is aware of a foreboding presence of Maw in the house that haunts and controls everybody especially the men. Maw is present in form of two elms that protect and subdue. They have a "sinister maternity "with the tears coming down when it rains (Batra; DUE 77). This sets the tone of the play which is sad, painful and degrading the maternal instincts into something sinister and suffocating.

It also indicates male chauvinistic mentality that relates tears to womanhood. Unaware of Maw's stronghold Ephraim Cabot thinks he can avoid her but her matriarchal stronghold is felt through the play as Eben wants to avenge his mother's death. Ephraim Cabot is forced to find solace in barn and others fear going into her room as her unsettling almost fearful energy pervades the house and the character's lives thereby making her lingering presence imposing.

The males all go to a common whore, Minnie, but keep insulting her as they treat her as a mere sex object. Simeon, Ephraim Cabot's son from first wife, mourns his dead wife as he simply misses her physical attributes not her warmth or love. The reactions of Ephraim Cabot's son Eben, Simeon and Peter, when they get to know that their father has remarried Abbie are quite unsettling. The half-brothers jokingly express their want to rape her. These sexualized invectives underline their sexist attitudes.

Abbie is cunning, shrewd and calculating as she very easily gains control over her dictatorial husband. She manipulates Ephraim Cabot into giving her the farm if she bears him a son. Ephraim Cabot is extremely dismissive of Abbie but that doesn't stop her from speaking her mind out. Cabot says, "A hum's got t' hev a woman". To which Abbie responds, "… (her voice taking possession) A woman's got t' hev a hum!" (Batra; DUE 108) Eben's softness and sensitivity is credited to his "dumb fool" mother. Another instance when Cabot sees Abbie only as a source for getting a son, he says: "Ye're on'y a woman. ABBIE--I'm yo're wife. CABOT--That hain't me. A son is me--my blood--mine. Mine ought t' git mine." (Batra; DUE 130).

She also successfully seduces Eben and despite her motive, she falls in love with Eben. When Abbie in a fit of rage, in order to prove her love for Eben, impulsively kills her newborn son, she accepts her error but the men in the play don't as it is against their ego to accept their mistake. Eben believes her and decides to share her fate. According to William Meredith Dawson, Abbie lives for physical gratification. In fact, her relationship with Eben is all about sensual gratification. Meredith Dawson claims that she is the "embodiment of evil as well as a destroyer of men since Abbie will stop at nothing to satisfy her own desires" (81). She also accuses her that "Lying, adultery, infanticide-these are the main stations of the will to power which motivate her. The men are pawns in her life to be used to her own advantage (81).

Clifford Leech explains vividly the need to possess the land, home and body. Ephraim finds it in his farm and its animals while Eben and Abbie find it in each other (40). Minnie, Maw and Abbie are all victims of the sexual stereotype. They are only seen as investment by males as they are meant to be possessed, fought over and ploughed like land. However, the females wield power and easily outmaneuver these abuse-hurling dismissive males.

SUBALTERNITY IN THE GREAT GOD BROWN

The Great God Brown is a play that rightly captures the essence of the age in a very unconventional way. Early twentieth century was a time of commercialization as well as materialism and O'Neill found himself in the middle of it. Virginia Floyd has rightly remarked that O'Neill's contempt of commercialism bordered on obsession (25). Dion hates the philistine society that made him adopt the mask and become somebody he is not. Edmond Gagey has found the play obtuse and evading analysis. He says that the play, "almost defies analysis" (53). Eugene O'Neill scorned at the greed and avarice that commercialization brought about that he himself said in an interview, Eugene O'Neill found this soul-sickening gruesome materialism quite pervasive which he demonstrated through Dion's character, a sensitive artist and William Brown, insensitive businessman who uses and abuses Dion's creativity to finally usurp his identity. Simply put a discord is shown between middle class businessman mentality and free-spirited creative artist.

Brown therefore represents the middle-class hostile attitude towards art and the artist and also the hollow superficial businessman who is uncreative. The play is also a tug of war between artistic ambition and business success. They are like the two sides of a coin wherein one represents the yin and other yang. Even Cybel, the prostitute whom both visit, seems to assert this idea when she says to Dion, "You're brothers, I guess, somehow" (O'Neill 50). Later, even Brown accepts it and adds,

"We're getting to be like twins" (O'Neill 87). The society and its standards put shackles on Dion's creativity and he becomes rakish and contemptuous. The change in his mask from Pan-like to Mephistophelean is clearly visible. He yearns to be an artist and squanders the money he got from the sale of his share of the company. Later, he is hired by Brown to ghost-design the blueprints. Here again he is traumatized by the market demands he says for Brown: "He hands me one mathematically correct barn after another and I doctor them up with cute allurements so that fools will desire to buy, sell, breed, sleep, love, hate, curse and pray in them!". Justifyin as to why he does all that he says, "I do this with devilish cleverness to their entire delight! Once I dreamed of painting wind on the sea and the skimming flight of cloud shadows over the tops of trees! Now . . ." (O'Neill 49-50).

As Falk asserts:- "... the cathedral is clear evidence that the inhibiting pressures of self-hatred and of society have distorted the spontaneous creative process into artificial grotesque parody of itself." (102). O'Neill imbued Dion with a poetic sensitivity and the inherent ability to self-destruct due to frustration brought out by the societal pressures (Clark171). These demands finally take a toll on the sensitive artist and he dies.

Brown earlier did not wear a mask because he had no inner self to hide. He was as said by Dion, "capable, college-bred American business man, boyish still and with the same engaging personality" (O'Neill 33). The myth of the American Dream takes a nosedive as Brown, who takes Dion's mask before he dies, now becomes Dion Brown. But he is neither true to himself nor to Dion's wife and children. Cybel highlights the art and nature but for Brown it is a commodity that has to be bought and possessed. This represents commercial exploitation of nature as well as capitalistic hubris. Brown considers her as a property to own but for Dion she is pure Mother Earth who is the ultimate force of life. It is not only Cybel that Brown wants to possess but also the creative talents of Dion that's why he puts his signature on all the designs made by Dion. Bogard has accurately stated about Brown that he is, "the secure God of a materialistic society, an assured possessor of all he surveys." (275).

Brown is a compete embodiment of a soulless society that like a slow poison feed on the artistic talents and ultimately devour their last shreds of artistic inspirations. In a way, even Brown is a victim of the smug middle-class culture that is startled by the eccentricities of a full life. Brown's parents are also a typical example of a middle-class family that wants their son to take up architecture as a profession not for its artistic joy but as a money earning business that will upgrade their social status. It will help them climb up the social ladder and look more dignified. So, no matter how many stoop-shouldered draftsmen he employs his designs will remain cold and tomb-like. After this Brown reveals his own face and says with self-skepticism: "Why must the demon in me pander to cheapness--then punish me with self-loathing and life-hatred? Why am I not strong enough to perish--or blind enough to be content?" (O'Neill 84).

Dion's mask is taking a toll on Brown as it has become more like Dion. Brown feels the pain of an artist but not the joy of creativity. Brown is aware of his childhood impertinence towards Dion but the societal pressure to accept his fault and eat a humble pie catches up with him. The irony is that Brown too in the end is destroyed by the society of which he is an integral part. For their superficial self-satisfaction and in order to sleep well the society must "…find a victim! They've got to quiet their fears, to cast out their devils, or they'll never sleep soundly again!" (O'Neill 92). Brown is the victim of the very society he represents as he is snuffed out and hounded by them once he steps onto the creative realm.

Eugene O'Neill therefore sends a strong message that condemns the culture, which is responsible for torturing the visionary and the ignorant. All the characters seem to be victims of a society that endorses complacency and materialism. He shows how this culture is self-destructive and leads to the devastation of artistic impulse by the unwarranted commercialization. The Babbitt-like subservience that is shown by Brown stunts his growth. His economic success makes him incapable of affirming to life. The mechanical society is oblivious of its own damaging tendencies as it is bereft of coherence with the natural world.

Eugene O'Neill ensured that he highlights the underdog and marginal so that the society understands how its judgmental eye makes the entire race live a double life in order to fit in. Girish Karnad tried to do the same thing with his plays. This was his way of making people aware of the societal problems and the undue pressure on an individual to be somebody they are not.

GIRISH KARNAD: SUBALTERN CONCERNS

Girish Karnad's three plays *Yayati, Hayavadana* and *Naga-Mandala* deal with the cultural forces that try to put an individual in a class defined societal role. These marginalized sections are primarily based on gender and class. Girish Karnad found this to be a fascinating opportunity to investigate the intersections of caste and gender. Cosimo Zene remarks are quoted in Kendre Vitthal's thesis titled "The Sense of History and Tradition in the Plays of Girish Karnad in The Light of Subaltern Perspective" as he laments the condition of Indian Subalterns in his article. She is concerned about the ideology at the basis of Subalternity which reduces dalit life to less than a human saying that "For them Subalternity becomes a spatial/territorial, economic, social, educational, and, above all, religious/ontological segregation (Kendre 23)".

Myths and legends are supposed to glorify the upper caste and vilify the lower as the latter are usually presented as demons, witches, tyrants or an embodiment of evil. Girish Karnad refashions myth in a way that the gendered subaltern emerges out of a shadowed gloom. The subalterns are a product of entrenched patriarchy and the societal standards of an ideal woman. Highlighting the importance of retelling the myths Aparna Bhargav Dharwadker explicates that the historical and muthical plays from the post-independence period depict the nation in the present but represent the pre-independence phase, but "the full complexity of this symbolic identification emerges only in contradistinction to colonial views of —the Indian past" in order to "to scrutinize the dominant tradition in the context of a pluralistic nation" (170).

SUBALTERNITY IN *YAYATI*

Yayati is Girish Karnad's version from an episode in The *Mahabharata*. Instead of glorifying the son's sacrifice the plays deals with web of caste and gender relations. The women in the play disrupt the male world by questioning and putting forward their opinions. Right from the beginning the Sutradhara gives an insight into turning the ancient myth on its head because the past lurks through the contemporary hopes, dreams and desires. The women wrestle in the male bigoted system to make themselves heard Sharmishtha and the minor character Swarnalata epitomize two kinds of approaches. Sharmishtha has grey shades while Swarnalata is assertive as a humble servant of Devayani. Sharmishtha is hounded for her caste and receives little understanding from others. She admits, "I do have tears in my eyes. But the world only cares for the embers there" (Karnad; YAYA 20). Devayani belongs to an upper caste and makes her presence known through her inherent caste superiority. Chitralekha vehemently opposes patriarchy and loses her life which makes Yayati realize that decrepitude and old age are inevitable.

The men seem to be worried about themselves and guise their demands as they are doing the entire kingdom some good. Yayati for his selfish motives wants to stay young but argues his case on the grounds of public service. He says, "This is not merely a question of an individual. We are talking of the future of our entire people" (Karnad; YAYA 65). Same is for Pooru who is trying to find his own identity but is disguising it as his inability to be as grand as his ancestors. The society mandates that a prince must rise up to the occasion and accept his responsibility to create and manage a great kingdom.

The plays central conflict is between two friends turned enemies Devayani, an upper caste, and the lower caste, Sharmishtha. Their relationship is very tortured that has underpinnings of caste and gender. Sharmishtha is a *Rakshasi* princess but belongs to a low caste and

Devayani belongs to an upper caste. Sharmishtha is enslaved by her father's word and continues to wreak havoc in Devayani's life with her scathing comments and vituperation. She is in a double bind as she is not only a slave but also a *Rakshasi*. Swarnlata, Devayani's maid, keeps on refereeing to her as a "satanic", "spiteful whore" who must be sent back to her tribe (Karnad; YAYA 7). Instead of standing in solidarity, these women continue to carry out vicious barbs against each other all based on caste divide, jealousy, frustration and vengeance. Sharmishtha herself admits to her *Rakshasi* antics, she says, "I promise you, madam, I was not being deliberately nasty. It is just that I am an uncouth *rakshasi*. And the situation here…a kshatriya palace ruled over by a Brahmin queen! Confusing isn't the word." (Karnad; YAYA 9).

Devayani is an upper caste who marries a kshatriya king because of the Kachas curse and Sharmishtha ensures that she is reminded of it every now and then through her piercing taunts. She never misses a chance to make Devayani feel that the basis of her marriage to Yayati is flawed. This clearly highlights the fact that Devayani's marriage was an arrangement to gain immortality. Sharmistha is a *Rakshasi* princess and spitefully reminds Devayani of her high stature, she says that she had everything including beauty, education, wealth, except birth- "an arya pedigree" (10). She goes on introspecting and self-assessing- "What was your worth? That your father knew the 'sanjeevani' spell. That is all…I opened my eyes. You had become the queen the Arya race, wife of King Yayati. And I was your slave" (Karnad; YAYA 10).

It is due to this dignity that in the beginning we see Sharmishtha spewing venom in order to assuage her humiliation. These acts of defiance highlight her as a subaltern looking for places to voice her opinion. It is through Sharmishtha's sarcastic interrogations that one gets to see how the males subjugate the females for their own gains. Sharmishtha herself is a victim of her father's order, which was given to keep Devayani's father, Sage Shukracharya, in his kingdom along with his precious knowledge of reviving the dead as Sharmishtha had humiliated both the father and daughter. Sharmishtha therefore, became a pawn as she explains her predicament to Yayati, "Devyani has her father's word that I shall be her slave. My father has given her father word that I shall be her slave. And I have given my father word that it shall be so." (Karnad; YAYA 17)

Earlier both Devayani and Sharmishtha were friends. One day their clothes were exchanged and Devayani citing her racial superiority condescendingly told Sharmishtha that, "You poor people. You only have to get into a piece of Arya attire. And you start fantasizing" (Karnad; YAYA 20). This wounded her pride so much that Sharmishtha out of spite pushed her into a well and left her there. This tarnished their relationship and sowed the seeds of their diatribes and hostility. So, she admits that though dhe finds it futile, yet strives to retrieve a part of her original self. She finds it difficult to escape this degredation- "The louder I scream, the more I declare myself a slave. That is the point. I have decided to turn myself into a performing freak (Karnad ; YAYA 18).

Pooru's dead mother is yet another *Rakshashi* woman to assert her identity and her deliberate plan to contaminate the *Bharatas* pure blood with *Rakshaha*. She confesses her plan to Yayati before she dies and Yayati explains it to Pooru thus, "She was a rakshasa woman and the Aryas had destroyed her home and hearth. She was bent on vengeance and the inferno she had created was her way of celebrating her success. She had made sure that the Crown prince of the Bharatas had rakshasa blood in him" (Karnad; YAYA 40). She is manifestation of a repressed rage that is brought out by suppression and disempowerment.

Another empowered woman is Chitraleka who is a collateral damage in Yayati's bid to stay young. She is Pooru's wife who questions patriarchy and instead of bowing down to it commits suicide, as there is lack of choice for her. She doesn't comply to Yayati's order of welcoming the old and decrepit Pooru to her bed chamber and in turn demands that since Yayati has taken Pooru's youth he must impregnate her. Her feisty nature shatters Yayati's pretensions with her corrosive questions. When Yayati reminds her of her marital vows of staying with Pooru she vehemently refutes his claims. Chitralekha flares up in defense and says, "I did not push him to the edge of the pyre, sir. You did. You hold forth on my wifely duties. What about your duty to your son? Did you think twice before foisting your troubles on a pliant son?" (62). When Yayati shauts her name, Chitralekha is bold enough to counter him saying- "Only my husband has the right to come in here without my permission. Or to shout my name when he pleases. I am not aware I have allowed anyone else that freedom", which obliges Yayati apologize to her (Karnad; YAYA 62).

Frustrated and dejected she exclaims, "You have your youth. Prince Pooru has his old age. Where do I fit in?" (Karnad; YAYA 62). This shows her identity's erasure. Women around the world who find themselves in the doldrums face this situation of not belonging. Chirtalekha commits suicide instead of succumbing to the overbearing demands of a patriarchal society. Her character has left an indelible mark on all its readers. Vitthal Kendre in thesis titled "The Sense of History and Tradition in the Plays of Girish Karnad In "The Light Of Subaltern Perspective" quotes Aparna Dharwadker who asserts that striking and memorable feature of that striking and memorable feature of Yayati is "its quartet of sentient, articulate, embittered women" who are subject to the male discretion and dominance in varied form. But at the heart of it remains their "success in subverting the male world through an assertion of their own rights and privileges" (Kendre 32).

Yayati through Sharmishtha, Devayani and Chitralekha bring out the angst, anger and frustrations of women in a male dominated society and of females who are in a double bind not because of gender but of caste as well. At last, it is Sharmishtha and Chitralekha that make Yayati accept his fate and give back Pooru his youth thereby highlighting the fact that Chitralekha's sacrifice did not go waste.

SUBALTERNITY IN *HAYAVADANA*

Hayavadana revolves around the triad of Padmini, Kapila and Devadatta. It is based on a folk-tale from *Kathasaritsagara* and from *Transposed Heads* by Thomas Mann. As Girish Karnad grew watching *Yashagana* performances, so he included devices from this folk genre. The narrator, Bhagavata, is essential as it adds a different layer of meaning to the female sexuality and the patriarchal framework. Girish Karnad tries to interrogate the traditional notion of femininity and seem to subvert and refashion the dominant narrative. As has been claimed by Girish Karnad himself in his Introduction to the Three Plays he says, as quoted in Vitthal Kendre's Thesis titled "The Sense of History and Tradition in the Plays of Girish Karnad "In the Light of Subaltern Perspective" asserts that while folk theatre seems to hold traditional values, it questions them at the same time. The mixing of human and non-human world and the interventions like chorus and masks "the simultaneous presentation of alternative points of view, of alternative attitudes to the central problem" (Kendre 39).

Karnda's usage of dolls and female chorus brings out Padmini's latent desires. Padmini doesn't want to be tied to one person as she wants variety of experiences and the female chorus state the main problem of the play in its beginning quoted in Kendre Vitthal thesis titled "The Sense of History and Tradition in the Plays of Girish Karnad "In the Light Of Subaltern Perspective", "Why should love stick to the sap of a single body? When the stem is drunk with the thick yearning of the many-petalled, many-flowered lantana, why should it be tied down to the relation of a single flower?" (Kendre 42).

Once married, Girish Karnad draws parallels with *Rama, Sita* and *Lakshmana* thereby giving a dialogic context for reference. Padmini has to be an embodiment of *Sita* that demands complete acquiescence to the patriarchy and society defined wifely roles. It is not only Padmini but also Hayavadana's mother who is a transgression to the societal *Sita* roles. She chooses a stallion to be her husband. This wilfulness is a threat to patriarchy.

Padmini who has her main door engraved with a two-headed bird is also a continuation of that unbridled female energy as was shown by Hayavadana's mother. Padmini desires Kapila for his physical vigour as compared to Devadatta who is more intellectual.

This pent-up sexual energy is the reason for the Ujjain fiasco that is the turning point of the play. Both Devadatta and Kapila commit suicide leaving Padmini abandoned and in a completely helpless situation.

Looking at her misery Goddess *Kali* grants her wish and asks her to join their heads to the body so that they can be brought to life again but Padmini mixes the heads. This switching of heads could be because of her latent desires, as she wanted Kapila's body and Devadatta's intellect. It is quoted in the play that Padmini, "…in her excitement she mixes them up" (Karnad; HAYA 103). Now the head of Devadatta is attached to Kapilas body and vice versa. However, Goddess *Kali* adds, "My dear daughter there should be a limit even to Honesty" (Karnad; HAYA 103). This transgressive act of honesty reveals dissent against patriarchy and sanctifies Padmini's sexual desire as she secures divine blessing from Goddess *Kali*. Since all this happened owing to Goddess *Kali's* intervention.

Through Padmini's act of transposition of heads and the divine intervention, both Devadatta and Kapila are indeed reborn since they partake in a song singing and laughing, they all sing, "What a good mix! No more tricks! Is this one that Or that one this? Ho! Ho!" (Karnad; HAYA 105). This happiness is short lived as Devadatta with Kapila's body resumes his earlier sophistication and flabbiness and Kapila with Devadatta's body regains his sturdy and muscular stature. This now adds misery to Padmini's life since everything again comes to haunt and torture her. So, she gives vent to her emotions through the lullabies she sings to her son, "Here comes a rider! From what land does he come? On his head a turban with a long pearly tail…." (Karnad; HAYA 117).

Padmini seems to represent the state of every woman who finds herself in a loveless marriage and whose emotions chock inside her. It is through the help of dolls that one actually gets to know about the hidden recesses of Pamini's mind when she is dreaming. They relay to us Padmini's persistent desire for Kapila's body. The phallic images in her dreams further symbolise her thirst and yearning for Kapila's body.

Padmini is the only constant as she is a witness to the change of men in her life. This traumatizes her to the extent that in agony she cries out, "Change! Change! Change! Change! Change! The sand trickles. The water fills the pot. And the moon goes on swinging, swinging, swinging from light to darkness to light." (Karnad; HAYA 119). Padmini feels unaccommodated and left out as her desires are trampled and brutally crushed. However, the dolls have been a witness to Padmini's dream and know her secret, who act as the ruthless society that judges a person vehemently. They comment on the prospect if her desires are to be made public, they say, "Doll II: She wants new dolls / Doll / I: The whore / Doll II: The bitch / Doll I: May her house burn down / Doll II: May her teeth fall out…Doll I: (To Devadatta) You wretch – before you throw us out watch out for yourself (Karnad; HAYA 121).

Unable to wrap her head around this change she wishes to go to the forest and find Kapila. Disregarding the societal censure, she defiantly goes to forest in search for Kapila. These vigorous and dynamic emotions are remarkably captured by the female chorus and represented as, "The river only feels the Pull of the waterfall. She giggles, and tickles the rushes on the banks, then turns. A top of dry leaves…Sings, tosses, leaps and sweeps on in a rush." (Karnad; HAYA 127). Compared to Padmini's flaring emotions Devadatta and Kapila look unperturbed and fail to match her energy and vitality. Since, both are on a path that would lead them to their graves, as they don't want to share and have no solution but to fight it out. Both die again leaving Padmini alone, abandoned and unfulfilled.

Aparna Dharwadker recognizes and acknowledges the fact that in the play though men kill themselves twice for a woman but her predicament is still the same as she is left yearning for completeness. She explains, "In the upside-down anti-patriarchal world of the Sanskrit folktale, as retold by Mann and Girish Karnad in the twentieth century, the men kill themselves twice for the sake of the woman." (339). Padmini doesn't want anybody else to write her story so she performs *Sati* not out of reverence for the men but because she wants to assert her identity and be one with the man she desires. This is an act of dissent against the patriarchy as she honours her extra-marital quest of sexual fulfilment. The rebellious but calamitous fate of Padmini reinforces her sexual quest and open defiance of patriarchy.

Hayavadana represents the conflict between societal traditions and an individual. Padmini wasn't considered a human but an ideal woman who had to strictly follow rules laid down by the male dominated society. Her unbeaten attitude for sexual completeness and the ambiguous societal attitude is meticulously represented. Ashley cohesively lists all the binaries that make up a subaltern:

When the binaries of body/head, intellect/emotion evolve, women empathised with the black / working / Dalit men in their attempt to resist the intellectual dominance of the whore/bourgeois / Brahmin man who established their power through cultural hegemony. It is axial and not natural. Now a woman might also agree with the notion of the perfect man because she has been trained through entertainment and other cultural devices to even dream in a set pattern. The autobiographical element classes with the historical, as the attempt are to explore those mutually exclusive ways (178).

He keenly observes, "Padmin is patronising of Devadutta and Kapila in different ways, by discounting them off their sexualities or attaching a change in them, makes her the powerful centre of the play" (179).

SUBALTERNITY IN *NAGAMANDALA*

Nagamandala expresses the defiance of a subjugated and marginalized female, Rani. Appanna remains callously unresponsive to the plight of his newlywed wife. Rani's expression of female desire is triumphantly celebrated as she manages to corrode male dominated society. In the beginning itself flames were personified and endowed with female voices. They had a candid carefree and uninhibited discussion.

These Flames act as choric commentators who narrate not only an insider's view point but also prove that human's view point is not the ultimate truth. Another discussion of the flames leads to the story of an old lady who had kept a *story* and *song* to herself thereby choking them but one day while she was snoring, they leapt out of her and the *story* took the shape of a woman and *song* became her sari. This showcases the repressed desires, disapproval of garrulity and wretched submission to authority.Rani's story brings to foreground all the females whose voices have been repressed and whose life is limited to the four walls of the house. Rani, that means queen, is subjected to an indifferent and cold behaviour by her husband Appanna whose very name means any man. So, Rani's story could be of any girl who has been shackled by patriarchy. Rani being a victim of a loveless marriage sees her husband only during the afternoons when he comes to bathe and have lunch. He locks her up before leaving to meet his concubine. Rani is a victim to a stifling loneliness and isolation as Appanna locks her up every day before leaving. She is forced to spend her monotonous days and nights in complete isolation, as she has no chance to mingle or visit someone. This patriarchal tyranny does not let any latent desires to find expression. Keeping women busy in domestic chores and making her aspire for the ideal wife parameters are only ways to keep women fettered.

Rani can now only dream about being carried away by eagle to reunite with her parents under an emerald tree. Not only this, she also dreams of a stag signifying a prince to rescue her from her martial misery. These repressed desires of meeting her parents or wishing for an ideal husband indicate her mental agony. Instead, she gets a demonic brute like Appanna and there is no reprieve for her misery. These fabricated fantasies help Rani survive and give momentary relief to her from her miserable marriage. Kurudavva provides an escape to Rani to entice Appanna by giving him a paste of magical roots. She agrees but is reluctant in giving him the paste so she pours it onto an anthill in fear of upsetting Appanna. However, Appanna is upset and slaps her to circumscribe her duties within the domestic sphere and establish himself as a dominant male figure. This also shows a submissive acceptance of violence as part of her wifely duties.

Little does Rani realise that a shape shifting *naga* lives in the anthill who after getting the paste poured becomes completely smitten by Rani. He takes the form her husband and embodies an ideal husband figure that Rani had been dreaming of. They consummate their marriage and enjoy conjugal bliss. *Naga* loves her immensely and ensures that they have a love-filled relationship in comparison to Appanna's monosyllabic responses. She enjoys complete marital bliss and *naga* showers her with not only love but also gives her the much-deserved respect.

Rani unquestioningly enjoys her time with *naga* who in the form of her husband gives her ultimate emotional and physical satisfaction in contrast to violent and inconsiderate Appanna. Rani doesn't want to accept the truth and only thinks of *naga* as Appanna however, the narrator flame doesn't think so. Rani discovers that she is pregnant and *naga* receives the news rather blankly and Appanna questions Rani fidelity and integrity. Unleashing his typical chauvinistic violence, he said as quoted in Vitthal

This enrages Appanna to the extent that he asks her to undergo a chastity test by holding the cobra in her hand and we see how finely and beautifully Rani has changed from being a submissive wife to a fiery married woman. She holds the cobra in her hand unperturbed and says, "I have held by this hand only two...My husband and... And this Cobra." (Karnad; NAGA 58).

The mockery of the trial and chastity test as well as the male dominated society that makes a woman undergo such tests in order to prove her intentions as well as her character. Her infidelity gives her a divine identity. The elders ensure that Appanna abjectly surrenders to Rani's new found divinity. Rani enjoys a full and happy life with a devoted husband, a son and Appanna's concubine as her servant. Moutushi Chakravartee comments, "Rani's attainment of divinity does not jar. Her adultery seems the proper lesson for her adulterous husband. As a powerful mode of expression, drama integrates within it, the fantasies of human mind" (185).

Eugene O'Neill's and Girish Karnad's plays critique the caste and class concerns as well as patriarchal dominance. It brings to forefront subaltern female characters. With great incisiveness, they probe deeper into subjugation of females by refashioning the myth in a way that it has become a timeless mouthpiece of female fierceness. Eugene O'Neill gives a fresh perspective to the class struggles in an industrialized society where the gap between the rich and poor is clearly visible. The crassness with which the working class is treated is vividly represented through the deplorable work conditions and their comparison to mere animals. He also stresses upon the ills of materialism that make men take part in an unending rat race that only leads to self-annihilation. Giving a modern insight into the plight of women O'Neill tries to give justice to his female characters.

Girish Karnad has presented an astute outlook of caste and gender with his sparkling and cutting sarcasm. Female subjugation is the most prevalent form of subalterns. The ideological paradigm of a docile and submissive wife is turned on its head and the females are brought out in a new light. Girish Karnad's plays try to recover the lost female voices so as to puncture established narratives and carve out the way to articulate female concerns in a cacophony of voices so as to move towards an inclusive approach. Girish Karnad to say in the words of Guha very adroitly amplifies the "small voices" which is negated by dominant patriarchal discourses.

Girish Karnad represents this patriarchal disregard for females, lack of documentation through his subversive use of folk-tales and myths. It is through these myths, and folk tales the voice of the subaltern is heard. As it has been rightly said by A.K. Ramanujan, "Folk materials also comment continually on official and orthodox views and practices in India...here, if we listen, we can hear the voice of what is fashionably called the subaltern—the woman, the peasant, the no literate, those who are marginal to the courts of kings and offices of the bureaucrats, the centres of power" (548). Looking at the subjugation of women at the hands of men one can draw parallels to Simon De Beauvoir comments that man defines woman not in herself but as relative to him; she is not regarded as an autonomous being... she is the incidental, the inessential as opposed to the essential. He is the subject, he is the absolute she is the other.

CONCLUSION

Drama aims to hold up a mirror to society. Ancient stories, combined with the eternal pursuit for self and the enslavement of the subaltern, have long been a theme for all kinds of plays. Eugene O'Neill and Girish Karnad perfected the art of highlighting the modern man's skirmishes with the self and the society. They used recurring themes of ancient myths, identity, and subjugation of the weak by vividly showcasing their characters trying to break the impasse.

Eugene O'Neill's plays were written from a very personal viewpoint. They mirrored the savage scars left by his family's complex and tragic connection. All of this created a dichotomy in Eugene's mind, which contributed to his highly intimate and dramatic writing style. Eugene O'Neill's writing during the nineteen twenties had hints of materialism however, key feelings based in spiritualism were brought to the forefront and augmented. Digging deeper into the skirmishes of the mind Eugene O'Neill ensured he reached a point where human soul lay shrouded under the layers of insecurity. He tried to understand and comprehend the reason behind one's passion, internal turmoil as well as identity issues. By doing so Eugene O'Neill writ his name in the galaxy of American writers who ensured that American drama had its own identity.

Girish Karnad, the son of a wealthy and accomplished physician, was exposed to wandering groups of players known as *Natak* companies or *Mandali's*. It left an unforgettable impression on his mind and piqued his curiosity. Girish Karnad's journey from Karnataka's *Natak Mandali* to Mumbai's captivating theatre inspired him to take playwriting seriously. Being born into a loving home it was difficult for Girish Karnad to study abroad. His filial love and accompanying obligations weighed him down and he eventually started pouring it out on paper and much to his own surprise it was a play that he wrote instead of his aim of taking up poetry. Kannada was his preferred language, and it was through it that he showcased the present as a kaleidoscope of the past. His writing endeavours drew on the living age and theatre. He looked for and defined

'*Indianness*' in drama, and highlighted drama that mirrored Indian customs.

The transcendental element of playwrights' works allows the present to peak through the veils of antiquity. The characters are etched out from the present-day people who seem to be conscious of their circumstances, situations and their roots. Eugene O'Neill worked around reworking Greek myths so as to weave his own plot and Girish Karnad ensured he used myths so as to add a touch of modernity to place his plays in the current scenario. Both mix contemporary characters into modern philosophical ideas to create a new interpretation for a new generation of readers. The heroes are annihilated as a result of their tragic flaw. When reading works by both playwrights, echoes and reverberation of Soren Kierkegaard, Friedrich Wilhelm Nietzsche, Martin Heidegger, Albert Camus, Jean- Paul Sartre, and Samuel Beckett can be found. Both playwrights' works have undertones of Existentialism. Eugene O'Neill and Girish Karnad are masters of immaculate writing, deploying commendable methods to take their audiences to this other realm. In their plays, relationships are inherently incongruous and chaotic. They make their characters yearn for love, but they rarely have a pleasant experience with it. The characters embark on an indefinite quest in which the troubles linger and the battle against them is never-ending. Death is the only method to eliminate the dilemma for the bulk of the characters.

Both playwrights touch on the existentialist, subaltern concerns, and mythopoeia concepts of the modernist movement, although in difference. Their plays employ expressionism's approaches and techniques in a distinct way, while the concept and spirit behind them is nearly identical. Existentialism is a modernist philosophy deduced from Martin Heidegger and Jean Paul Sartre that is highly and deeply linked with the precarious condition of the modern man, as well as his secluded and inconsequential existence in a materialistic, superficial, and capitalistic society in this chaotic and anarchic modern age ungoverned by anybody. The plays of Eugene O'Neill and Girish Karnad criticise patriarchal rule as well as caste and social concerns. It puts Subaltern female figures in the spotlight. They dive deeper into female enslavement and make their women feisty and inquisitive.

Eugene O'Neill brings out the stark gap in poor and rich thereby ensuring a fresh perspective is given to class struggles. The ruthlessness and crassness with which the working class is handled is demonstrated by the horrid, absolutely appalling working conditions as well as analogies drawn with animals. He also underscores the flaws of materialism, which force men to be what they are not and making them go on a downward spiral. Eugene O'Neill seeks to give his female characters' justice by giving a modern perspective to their struggles. One might find parallels between Simon De Beauvoir and the subjugation of women at the hands of men, "Man defines woman not in herself but as relative to him; she is not regarded as an autonomous being... she is the incidental, the inessential as opposed to the essential. He is the subject; he is the absolute - she is the other." (Beauvoir xvi)

The plays of Girish Karnad blend legendary narratives with expressionist techniques and methods. With his sparkling and piercing sarcasm, Girish Karnad has offered an insightful perspective of caste and gender. The most common form of subalterneity is the subjugation of women. By turning the ideal image of women on its head Girish Karnad raises a few pertinent questions on individuality and societal pressures. His plays attempt to reclaim lost female voices in order to disrupt conventional narratives and carve out a way to express female issues amidst a cacophony of voices so as to move towards a more inclusive approach. Girish Karnad, to use Guha's terminology, adroitly amplifies the "little voices" that are stifled and negated by patriarchal ideologies (3).

Eugene O'Neill and Girish Karnad's characters are highly contemporary, with sharp emotional reactions and understanding of the adverse circumstances. They are regular people who have been thrust into extraordinary circumstances. Yank, Ephraim, Dion, Appanna, Devadatta, and Pooru all represent distinct social classes. They feel intense rootlessness and are always on the quest for happiness. As seen in the cases of Yank and Dion, their despondency is based on either their heredity or their economic condition. The men are torn between wanting to be and not to be. Either to comply with the system and completely forget their inner self and perish in order to maintain their individuality.

Ephraim of *Desire Under Elms,* by Eugene O'Neill, has the same idiosyncrasies and quirks as Girish Karnad's titular character in *Yayati.* They both depict a highly ruthless and oppressive shadow patriarch who, in order to get what he wants, transforms into a merciless tyrant. Ephraim subjugates his wives and sons by making them spend all day in the field, while Yayati subjugates Sharmistha and Chitralekha by making them bow down to his whims. They wish to live forever and are unconcerned about death. Sons of both Ephraim and Yayati are also very similar. Both Eben and Pooru try to make up for their father's wrongdoings, but they become caught in the farrago and make hasty decisions that have a detrimental effect on their wives and lives. Ephraim marries a girl half his age, proving that he may still have a son at the age of seventy. Sukracharya, Yayati's father-in- law, curses him to old age in his prime after he is caught cheating on his wife, Devyani. Pooru, Yayati's son, is expected to take his curse in order to enjoy carnal pleasures. Girish Karnad reimagines the age-old narrative of a father and son swapping ages. Eugene O'Neill also reworks the Pheadra-Hippolytus myth and examines true love in *Desire Under Elms.* Both of them dramatize the plight of man, who, despite being comfortable, is continuously seeking for more and pursuing worldly bliss in vain. His attempt to materialistic happiness are not only hollow but also futile.

Yank from *The Hairy Ape* is another character worth considering, who in his search for identity not only loses his individuality but also his will to live. Yank is a mighty ship's stoker, but he comes face to face with reality when an affluent Mildred reminds him of his shabbiness and ugliness after she refers to him as an Ape. This Hairy Ape then embarks on a trip to discover his place in society, but finds himself irrevocably bound by society's dictates. He eventually perishes at the hands of an ape. They both appear to feel that human impulses lead to a calamity since man is battling his personal demons and internal duress's. The main cause of their unhappy life is the tangled web of connections from which they suffer and are eventually pushed into isolation. Their characters Yank, Yayati, Pooru, Ephraim, Appanna, Devdatta, and Eben serve as a wake-up call to those who blunder into tragedy simply to find their bearings.

The Great God Brown's Dion and Brown, Devadatta, and Kapila of *Hayavadana* are victims of estrangement and suffer as a result of their incompleteness. Brown and Kapila both fall for the wife of one of their friends, which leads to their doom. Dion and Devadatta are the characters that get caught up in the drudgery and humdrum of ordinary life. They are also subjected to the expectations of their family and friends. All male characters are troubled and haunted by rootlessness, alienation, and melancholy, making them feel hollow and unfinished. The more these characters struggle to establish their identity, the closer they get to their doom. In the tragic duel, Devadatta and Kapila die, and Padmini commits *Sati*. However, none of the three characters achieves their goals, highlighting the futility of a man's pursuit for completeness. Kirtinath Kurtkoti encapsulates the plight of characters in his introduction to Hayavadana, he says, "Neither the death of the lovers nor the subsequent *sati* of Padmini is presented as tragic; the death serves only to emphasise the logic behind the absurdity of the situation." (qtd. in Karnad 70).

The female characters represented by Eugene O'Neill and Girish Karnad are feisty, outspoken indulgent women who question and challenge the sanctity of nuptial ties. The majority of females indulge in extramarital affairs and have no qualms about it. For women, the search for meaning does not end with marriage, but rather intensifies.

Abbie is married to Ephraim in *Desire Under Elms*, but she falls in love with her stepson Eben and begets a son with him. Padmini is another self-indulgent character who begins her search for fulfilment only after she is married. Her search for a complete man who possesses both Devadatta and Kapila's traits exacerbates and aggravates her situation and compels all of them to become estranged and distant. In *Nagamandala,* Rani is a submissive and subservient wife at first, but she finds happiness in a shape-shifting *naga*. Rani spends her days with Appanna, her abusive husband, and her nights with *naga*, her lover.

Kurudavva is the one who encourages Rani to seek love in her relationship.

The women of Eugene O'Neill and Girish Karnad aren't the typical conservative husband-loving spouses; instead, they tend to follow their own whims and fancies. These characters appear to be yearning to spread their wings and fly to find their hidden self as well as their individuality right from the start. Despite the fact that they are married, they continue their hunt for the perfect man. When he creates his female characters, Eugene O'Neill considers how vital they are to the play, whether it's the affluent, spoilt child Mildred who rattles Yank's world in *The Hairy Ape* or the maternal Cybel in *The Great God Brown* who becomes a safe haven for distraught Dion. Eugene O'Neill has his females as an important catalyst in the play. Margaret is a faithful, loving wife in Eugene O'Neill's *The Great God Brown*, but she is also an ignorant, naive individual who accepts life's gifts without question. Abbie of *Desire Under the Elms*, on the other hand, is on the opposite end of the spectrum, and she approaches everything with care and caution.

When it comes to female characters, Girish Karnad is the one who has shattered the shackles of orthodoxy and forced these women to fight for what they want. Devayani, Chitralekha and Sharmishtha are shown to be pawns in the hands of men. None of them, however, accept patriarchy as a reality and accede to it. When Devayani discovers Yayati has slept with her nemesis Sharmishtha, she rejects her as a junior queen and abandons Yayati. Yayati's life choices are questioned by Sharmishtha, who makes him consider the consequences of swapping ages with his son. Pooru, Yayati's son, is Chitralekha's husband. Chitralekha questions patriarchy, moral standards, and societal responsibilities. When she learns that Pooru has decided to swap ages with his father, she invites Yayati to share the nuptial bed with her because Yayati is taking her husband's youth and must meet her emotional and physical needs. This enrages Yayati, and he tries to reason with her, but she commits suicide rather than cave into patriarchal forces.

Padmini of *Hayavadana* is another example of a woman who is put to the test to prove her worth in the face of patriarchal expectations. She is a lotus divided between two schisms, as her name suggests. She desires a perfect mix of brain and beauty, so she unwittingly swaps her husband's head with that of his friend, resulting in the athletic and agile Kapila's body and wisdom of Devadatta's head. Her pursuit, however, leads to her death since she feels incomplete and unfulfilled.

Eugene O'Neill and Girish Karnad put their characters in tough positions, then raise them like a phoenix, from the ashes to fight even better and harder. Male characters Yayati, Yank, Ephraim, Eben, Dion, Devadatta, Kapila, Brown, and Pooru, all unhappy and dissatisfied with their life, set the route for their eventual downfall. The female characters, on the other hand, struggle for their rights and, for the most part, succeed in achieving what they want, except for Padmini, who craved an absolute marriage of beauty and intelligence.

Even though Eugene O'Neill and Girish Karnad's plays drew significantly on myths and folklore, they were fully modern in spirit and attitude. They hid a remarkable intelligence and sensibility that connected not just with the plots, but also with the modern man, whose unabashed decay of ethics and moralities was depicted in his plays. In the complicated world of convoluted relationships, their characters strived for perfection and completeness. The plays swinging between traditional and modern, served as a mirror to society. They seem to have handled the important subject of identity adroitly, writing strong and heart-breaking plays full of spitfires of questions and volcanic emotional outbursts.

Girish Karnad specialises in what the French literary critic Genette refers to as transgeneric practise, which entails converting mythic, folk, and historical narratives into theatre. He adapts the plots from existing sources into new dramatic shapes. All of his plays are transpositions in this sense, in which the original storylines are reinterpreted using the aesthetic standards of a fundamentally other generic process. These works, reworked into a new form, constitute unique insight on life that is relevant to today's society. Girish Karnad draws plots from variety of sources because he believes they are pertinent and allow him to reflect upon present social and political life in a more nuanced and structured way. Many taboos and forbidden subjects exist in real life that cannot be openly discussed. Myth, folklore, and historical events/lives of historical personalities give him a broad canvass that allows him to express undesirable or prohibited views in a socially acceptable manner. Simply said, these adaptations can be used as smokescreen for one's criticism of socio - economic and political realities.

Eugene O'Neill's understanding of tragedy pushed him to a deep investigation of the human psyche. He agreed with the world's best writers that tragedy arises from primal human emotions and man's blind struggle with nature's forces within himself that he is unable to control. These forces have been given names in modern psychology. It is possible for Eugene O'Neill to provide a contemporary interpretation of the tragic action and the dilemma that ensues.

Using plays from the dramatic oeuvre of famed American playwright Eugene O' Neill and India's contemporary voice Girish Karnad, this study proposes pertinent questions about the character's pursuit of identity, subaltern issues, and the ways myths play a key role. The man and the creator are complementary in Eugene O'Neill's plays since the man has experienced hardships and the artist has given shape to the struggle.

Girish Karnad augments the modern times and perceptions by associating them to folklore, fables, and traditional Indian folklore. Reading both playwrights' works allows one to not only reflect on life, but also to conceive and comprehend the context and milieu of the writer and his time. The employment of myths to have a mirrored impact on society, the battle to abolish class disputes, and the question of identity all spurred heated debate and the playwrights struggled to find powerful insights to decipher the essence of it all.

These authors attempt to portray the world's anarchic state by contrasting it with the chaotic and enigmatic situations depicted in scenes that alternate between fantasy and reality, as well as by portraying characters who are fantastic and eccentric not only in themselves but also in their thoughts, visions, and moods. The plays by O'Neill and Girish

Karnad do not provide a resolution to the characters' problems, but it does provide solace and a consolation to the audience who believe they are not alone in this bizarre world. The characters' hardships and tribulations are unending and persistent, establishing the universal reality of a man's eternal yearning for belonging. For them, the journey is more vital than the destination, which is a cathartic experience. Myths assist the playwright in seeking answers to man's everlasting concern of finding a mooring by anchoring them to their past.

It is not only the playwrights who have been grappling with these concerns in this unfathomable universe, but also an individual. Underneath the social disarray and the vacant prattle of daily life, people are looking for identity, meaning, and the chance to express themselves. The current global pandemic reflects civilization in a harsh light, prompting one to recollect great romantic poet Wordsworth's rhetorical question, "What man has made of man?" (Wordsworth) In these challenging and trying times, the works of both playwrights peer down on us, opening our eyes to decades of a human being's loneliness, quest for self, mythic interconnections, and enslavement and subjugation of the underprivileged.

BIBLIOGRAPHY

Abrams, M.H.. *A Glossary of Literary Terms*. Singapore: Thomson Asia, 2003. Print. Alexander, Doris M. "Eugene O'Neill as Social Critic." *American Quarterly* 6.4 (1954):

349–63. Print.

---. *O'Neill's Creative Struggle: The Decisive Decade*. Pennsylvania: Pennsylvania State University Press, 1992. Print.

---. *The Tempering of Eugene O'Neill*. Harcourt, Brace & World, New York: 1952. Print.

Antush, John V. "Eugene O'Neill: Modern and Postmodern." *The Eugene O'Neill Review*

13.1, (1989): 14–26. *JSTOR*. Web. 25 May 2022

Ashcroft, Bill, Gareth Griffiths, and Helen Tiffin. *Post-Colonial Studies: The Key Concepts*. London: Routledge, 2013. Print.

Ashley, N.P. "Effacing Hayavadana: On the Masks of the Text. *Girish Karnad's Plays Performance and Critical Perspectives*. eds. Delhi: Pencraft, 2019. 187-189. Print.

Babu, M. Sarat. "The Concept of Chastity and *Nagamandala*". *The Plays of Girish Karnad: Critical Perspectives*. Eds. Jaydipsinh Dodiya, New Delhi: Prestige Books,1999. Print.

Batra, Shakti. *Eugene O'Neill's Desire Under Elms: A Critical Study*. Delhi: Surjeet, 2017.

Print.

---. *Eugene O'Neill's The Hairy Ape: A Critical Study with Complete Text, Explanatory Notes, Paraphrases And Questions With Answers*. Delhi: Surjeet, 2017. Print.

Beauvoir, Simone de. Trans. H.M. Parshley. "Introduction." *The Second Sex*. New York:Alfred A. Knopf, 1961. Print.

Bevinagidad, Basu. "The Awakened Woman in Yayati." Eds by Basavaraj Donur *New Perspectives on Girish Karnad's Plays*. Bengalore: Kanva, 2009. Print.

Bhadra, Gautam, Gyan Prakash, and Susie Tharu. *Subaltern Studies X: Writings on South Asian History and Society*. New Delhi: Oxford U Press, 1999. Print

Black, Stephen A. *Eugene O'Neill: Beyond Mourning and Tragedy*. Yale: New Haven,2002. Print.

Bloom, Steven F.. *Student Companion to Eugene O'Neill*. New York: Green PublishingGroup, 2007. Print.

Bogard, Travis. *Contour in Time The Plays of Eugene O 'Neill*. New York: The OxfordUniversity Press, 1972. Print.

Boulton, Marjorie. *The Anatomy of Drama*. New Delhi: Kalyani, 1985. Print.

Bowen, Croswell. *The Curse of the Misbegotten: A Tale of the House of O'Neill*. NewYork: McGraw-Hill, 1959. Print.

Bram, Leon L., Robert S. Phillips and Norma H. Dickey. *Funk & Wagnalls NewEncyclopedia*. New York, Funk & Wagnulls, 1979. Print.

Burian, Jarka M. "The Uses of Classical Myth in Modern Drama." *The Massachusetts Review* 11.2 (1970): 401–08. *JSTOR*. Web. 24 May 2022.

Campbell, Joseph. *The Hero With a Thousand Faces*. New York: Princeton, 1968.

Camus, Albert. (Trans.) Justin O 'Brien. *The Myth of Sisyphus*. New York: Knopf, 1957.

Print.

Cargill, Oscar et al. eds. *O 'Neill and His Plays Four Decades of Criticism*. New York:New York University, 1961. Print.

Carpenter, Frederic I.. *Eugene O'Neill*. UK: Brimstones, 1964. Print.

Chakravartee, Moutushi. "Myth and Reality in Hayavadana and Naganandala." *Girish Karnad's Plays Performance and Critical Perspectives*. ed. Tutun Mukherjee. Delhi: Penkraft, 2019. 184-189. Print.

Christopher, Lo. Etal. "A Needs-Based Perspective on Cultural Differences in IdentityFormation, Identity." *Research Gate* 11:3 (2011): 211-230. Web. 3 Feb 2020.

Churchwell, Sarah. "Eugene O'Neill: Master of American Theatre." *The Guardian*. 30March 2012. Web. 9 June 2021.

---. "Eugene O'Neill: The Dark Genius of American Theatre." *The Spectator*. 29 Nov 2014.

Web. 18 Aug 2021.

Clark, Barrett H. *Eugene O'Neill: The Man and His Plays*. New York: Robert M. McBrideand Co., 1929. Print.

Cole, Toby. *Playwrights on Play Writing: The Meaning and Making of Modern Drama from Ibsen to Ionesco*. New York: Hill and Wang. 1961. Print.

Cunningham, Frank R. "O'Neill's Beginnings and the Birth of Modernism in American Drama." *The Eugene O'Neill Review* 17.1/2 (1993): 11–20. *JSTOR. Web.*1 May. 2020.

Deng, Francis M.. *War of Visions: Conflict of Identities in the Sudan*. Washington:Brookings, 2011. Print.

Dharwadker, Aparna Bhargav. *Theatre of Independence: Drama Theory and UrbanPerformance in India since 1947*. Iowa: University of Iowa, 2005. Print.

Dharwadker, Vinay. "Indian Writing Today: A View from 1994." *World Literature Today*

68.2 (1994): 237–41. *JSTOR*. Web. 15 May. 2020.

Dhawan, R.K.. "Girish Karnad: The Man and the Writer." Eds. Jaydipsinh Dodiya. *The Plays of Girish Karnad: Critical Perspectives.* New Delhi: Prestige, 2009. Print.

Donur, Basavaraj. "A Duologue with Girish Karnad" eds in *New Perspectives on GirishKarnad's Plays.* Bengalore: Kanva, 2009. Print.

---. "Protest in the Plays of Karnad" eds in *New Perspectives on Girish Karnad's Plays.*

Bengalore: Kanva, 2009. Print.

Dutta, Amrita. "Defence Against the Dark Arts." *The Sunday Express.* 7 October 2018.

We. 11 June 2020.

Edith J.R. Isaacs, "Meet Eugene O'Neill." *Theatre Arts.* XXI (1916): 576-587. Web. 29January 2019.

Engel, Edwin A.. *The Haunted Heroes of Eugene O'Neill.* Harvard: Harvard University,1953. Print.

Fagin, N. Bryllion. "Eugene O'Neill." *The Antioch Review* 14.1 (1954): 14–26. *JSTOR.Web.*21 April 2020.

Falk, Doris. *Eugene O 'Neill and the Tragic Tension. An Interpretative Study of the Plays.*

New Brunswick: Rutgers University Press, 1958. Print.

Floyd, Virginia. *Eugene O' Neill: A World View.* New York: Frederick Unger, 1979. Print.

---. *The Plays of Eugene O'Neill: A New Assessment.* New York: Ungar, 1985. Print. Frye, Northrop. *The Great Code: The Bible and Literature.* New York: Toronto, 1982.

Print.

Gagey, Edmond. *The Revolution in American Drama.* New York: Columbia, 1947. Print.

George, Jose. "*Nagamandala*as a Folk/Fake Morality Play: A Study of the Folk Paradigm in Kamad's play in the Light of the Naga Cult of Kerala". *Girish Karnad's Plays Performance and Critical Perspectives.* (ed.) Tutun Mukherjee, New Delhi: Pen craft International, 2006. Print.

Ghani, Hana. "Mythic Plot and Character Development in Eugene O'Neill' *The Great Brown God.*" *Mustansiriyah Journal of Arts* 33 (2007): 1-22. Print.

Ghosh, Manomohan. *A Treatise on Ancient Indian Dramaturgy and Histrionics: Natyasastram Ascribed to Bharata Muni.*Varanasi: Chawkhambha, 2007. Print.

Gill, Virender Kumar. "The Crisis of Self-Identity in the Selected Works of EugeneO'Neill." *International Journal of English Research* 2.6 (2016): 70-71. Web. 13

August 2019.

Gleason, Philip. "Identifying Identity: A Semantic History." *Journal of American History*

6:9 (1983): 10–931. Print.

Goyal, B. S. *The Strategy of Survival: The Human Significance of Eugene O'Neill's Plays.*

Ghaziabad: Vimal Prakashan, 1975. Print.

Guha, Ranajit. *The Small Voice of History: Collected Essays.* New Delhi: PermanentBlack, 2009. Print.

---. "The Small Voice of History." *Subaltern Studies IX.* ed. Shahid Amin and DipeshChakravarty. New Delhi: Oxford,1996. Print.

Haberman, Donald. *The Plays of Thornton Wilder: A Critical Study.* Connecticut:Wesleyan University, 1967. Print.

Hall, Stuart. "Introduction: Who Needs 'Identity'?" eds. Straut Hall and Paul du Gay.

Questions of Cultura Identity. London: Sage, 1996. Print.

Hawley, John C. *Encyclopedia of Postcolonial Studies*. London: Greenwood Press, 2004.

Print.

Highsmith, James Milton. "The Cornell Letters: Eugene O'Neill on His Craftmanship To George Jean Nathan." *Modern Drama* (1973): 68-88. Print.

Hischak, T. S. (2004). The Oxford Companion to American Theatre. Oxford UniversityPress, p. 275.

"Identity." *Merriam Webster Dictionary.* 9 august 2020. Web. 18 July 2021.

<https://www.merriam-webster.com/dictionary/identity>.

"Identity." *Oxford Learners Dictionary.* We. 6 June 2020.

<https://www.oxfordlearnersdictionaries.com/definition/english/identity?q=IDE TITY>.

Jing, Jing, and Huo Feng-chun. "On Eugene O'Neill Inheritance to Greek Tragedy in *Desire Under the Elms*." *Journal of Literature and Art Studies* 5.11 (2015): 1042 1046. Print.

Joshipura, Pranav. "Nag-Mandala Reconsidered." *The Plays of Girish Karnad: Critical Perspectives*. Eds. Jaydipsinh Dodiya, New Delhi: Prestige Books, 1999. Print.

Kao, Wei H. "When Incest is Not a Taboo: Desire and the Land in Eugene O'Neill's *Desire Under the Elms* and Marina Carr's *On Raftery's Hill*." (2010):119-139.http://doi.org/10.6257/2010.5119

Kakar, Sudhir. *The Inner World The Indian Psyche*. Delhi: Oxford University Press, 1996.

Print.

Kapoor, Jaya. *The Dramatic Journey of Eugene O'Neill and Samuel Beckett.* Delhi:Partridge, 2020. Print.

Karnad, Girish. "Acrobating between the Traditional and the Modern." *Indian Literature*

32.3 (1989): 84–99. *JSTOR.*Web.13 May. 2020.

———

 Girish Karnad: The Fire and the Rain. New Delhi: Oxford University Press, 1998.

Print.

---. "Theatre in India." *Daedalus* 118.4 (1989): 330–52. *JSTOR.* Web.14 April.2020.

---. *Three Plays*. New Delhi: Oxford University, 1994. Print.

---. Yayati, New Delhi, Oxford University Press, 2008. Print.

Kendre Vitthal R. "The Sense of History and Tradition in the Plays of Girish Karnad In The Light Of Subaltern Perspective." PhD.Thesis. U. of Swami Ramanand TeerthMarathwada.2021.Print

Kurtkoti, Kirtinath. "Girish Karnad's First Play." Eds by Basavaraj Donur *New Perspectives on Girish Karnad's Plays*. Bengalore: Kanva, 2009. Print.

Kushner, Tony. "The Genius of O'Neill." *The Eugene O'Neill Review*, vol. 26, 2004, pp.

248–56. *JSTOR.* Web. 30 April. 2020.

Krutch, Joseph Wood. "Introduction." *Nine Plays by Eugene O'Neill* by Eugene O'Neill.

New York: Liveright, 1932. Print.

Lawson, John Howard."Eugene O'Neill." Ed. John Gassner. *O'Neill: A Collection ofCritical Essays*. New Jersey: Prentice-Hall, 1964. Print.

Leech, Clifford. *Eugene O'Neill*. New York: Grove, 1963. Print.

Leslie, Julia. "Nailed to the Past: Girish Karnad'' Plays." *Journal of South Asian Literature*

32.1 (1996): 50–84. *JSTOR*. Web. 13 June. 2020.

Loomba, Ania. *Colonialism and Postcolonialism*. London: Routledge, 2014. Print

Louai, El Habib. "Retracing the concept of the subaltern from Gramsci to Spivak: Historical developments and new applications." *African Journal of History and Culture* 4.1(2012): 4-8. Print.

Louis, Sheaffer. *O'Neill: Son and Playwright*. US: Cooper Square, 2002. Print.

Ludden, David. *Reading Subaltern Studies: Critical History, Contested Meaning and the Globalization of South Asia*. London: Anthem, 2011. Print.

Madden, David. *Introduction: True Believers, Atheists, and Agnostics in American Dreams, American Nightmares*. Carbondale and Edwardsville: Southern Illinois Univ, 1970. Print.

Mahfouz, Safi Mahmoud. "Tragic Passion, Romantic Eloquence, and Betrayal in Eugene O'Neill's *Desire Under the Elms*." *Studies in Literature and Language* 1.3 (2010):1-15. Print.

Malas, Abhinandan. "Gender Narratives and Cultural Perspectives in Girish Karnad's

Yayati, Hayavadana and *Naga-Mandala*." *The Criterion* 5 (2014): 12-20. Web. 29

September 2020.

Manheim, Michael. *Eugene O'Neill's New Language of Kinship*. New York: University Press, 1982. Print.

---. "The Great God Brown' in the Light of O'Neill's Last Plays." *The Eugene O'Neill Review*. 14.1/2 (1990): 5–15. *JSTOR*. Web. 25 May 2022.

Massa, Ann. *American Literature in Context: 1900-1930*. New York: Metheun and Company, 1982. Print.

McCown, Cynthia. "The Great God Brown: A Diagnostic of Commercialism's Ills." *The Eugene O'Neill Review* 17.1/2 (1993): 53–59. *JSTOR*. Web.18 May. 2020.

Merrill, Charles A. "Eugene O'Neill, World-Famous Dramatist, and Family Live in Abandoned Coast Guard Station on Cape Cod." Eds. *Conversations with Eugene O'Neill*. Jackson: Mississippi, 1990. Print.

Miller, Jordan. "Myth and the American Dream: O'Neill to Albee." *Modern Drama* 7.2 (1964): 190-198. Print.

Mishra, Jyoti. "A Critical Study of Cultural Ethos in Girish Karnad." PhD thesis. U of Jiwaji, 2016. Print.

"Modern Mythology." *Encyclopedia.* Web. 24 December 2018.

"Modern Mythology." Myths and Legends of the World. . *Encyclopedia.com.* 23 May.

2022 <https://www.encyclopedia.com>.

Mongia, Padmini. eds.. "Introduction." *Contemporary Postcolonial Theory: A Reader*.

Delhi: Oxford, 1997. 223-247. Print.

Mossman, Mark A. "Eugene O'Neill and 'the Myth of America': Ephraim Cabot as the American Adam." *The Eugene O'Neill Review* 23.1/2 (1999): 49–59. *JSTOR*. Web.24 May 2022.

Mukherjee, Tuntun. "A Conversation with Girish Karnad" *Girish Karnad's Plays Performance and Critical Perspectives.* (ed.) Tutun Mukherjee, New Delhi: Pen craft International, 2006. Print.

Eds. *Girish Karnad's Plays: Performance and Critical Perspectives.* Delhi: Penecraft,2012. Print.

Mundra, S.C.. *The Hairy Ape.* Bareily: Raja Barqui, 2004. Print.

"Myth." *Merriam-Webster.* Web. *https://www.merriam-webster.com/dictionary/myth*.

"Mythopoeia." *Tropedia.* Web. 16 Feb 2021.

https://tropedia.fandom.com/wiki/Mythopoeia

Nagarajan, M.S. "Girish Karnad Revisited." 27 June 2011. Web. 16 December 2018. Naik, M.K.. " From the Horse's Mouth: A study of *Hayavadana.*" (eds.) Tutun Mukherjee.

Girish Karnad's Plays Performance and Critical Perspectives. New Delhi:Penecraft, 2006. Print.

Naik, M.K. "Cinderella Still: Recent Indian English Drama" Littcrit. Volume 27, Number1&2, June-Dec. 2001.

Nandakumar, Prema. Rev. of "Karnad's Three Plays." *World Literature Today* 69.2(1995): 434–35. *JSTOR.* Web. 18 May. 2020.

Nayar, Pramod K. *Postcolonial Literature: An Introduction.* Delhi: Pearson Longman,2008. Print.

New World Encyclopaedia. 28 Dec 2012. Web. 11 Feb 2020.

https://www.newworldencyclopedia.org/entry/Drama

Nivedita, Sister and Ananda K. Coomaraswamy. *Myths and Legends of the Hindus andBuddhists.* Kolkata: Advaita Ashrama, 2001. Print.

Ohno, Kumi. "Eugene O'Neill's *The Great God Brown*: Dualism of the Mask." 5November 2019. Web. 26 August 2020.

O'Neill, Eugene. "Memoranda on Masks." *American Spectator* 1.1 (1932) Print.

---. *The Great God Brown: The Fountain, The Moon of the Caribbees, and Other Plays*.

New York: Boni Liveright, 1926. Print.

Ou, Hsin-Yun. "Classical, Biblical, and Shakespearean Intertextuality in Eugene O'Neill's *Desire under the Elms*. *The IAFOR International Conference on Arts & Humanities*. 2016. Web. 14 April 2021.

Pacheco, Gilda. "The Female Image in Eugene O'Neill's *Desire Under the Elms* and *A Moon for the Misbegotten*." *Filologia y Lingistica* XXI.1 (1995): 55-63. Web. 13 August 2020.

Porter, Thomas E. *Myth and Modern American Drama*. Detroit: Wayne State University, 1969. Print.

Prakash, Gyan. "Subaltern Studies as Postcolonial Criticism." *The American Historical Review* 99.5 (1994): 1475–90. *JSTOR*. Web 22 Apr. 2022.

Racey, Edgar. "Myth as Tragic Structure in *Desire Under the Elms*." *Modern Drama* 5.1 (1962): 42-46. Print.

Rachna. "Identity Crisis in Eugene O'Neill's *The Hairy Ape*." *New Man International Journal of Multidisciplinary Studies* 1.10 (2014): 26-33. Web. 11 December 2020.

Raghavacharyulu, D.V.K. *Eugene O'Neill A Study*. Bombay: Popular Prakasham, 1965.

Print.

Ramanujan, A.K. *The Collected Essays of A.K. Ramanujan*. ed. Vinay Dharwadker. New Delhi: Oxford, 2012. Print.

Rangan. V.. "Myth and Romance in *Nagmandala* or Their Subversion?" (eds.) Tutun Mukherjee. *Girish Karnad's Plays Performance and Critical Perspectives*. New Delhi: Penecraft, 2006. Print.

Rani, Padma & P. Hari. "The Form of Indian drama in English: A Few Problems." *IndianEnglish Drama: Critical Perspectives*. Eds. Dodiya, K. Jaydipsingh and Surendran,

K.V. New Delhi: Sarup and Sons, 2002. Print.

Rickett, Arthur Compton. *A History of English Literature*. New Delhi: Universal Book Stall, 1990. Print.

Saravanan, T. "Quest for Identity." *The Hindu* 20 Jan 2010. Web. 8 Aug 2020.Shakespeare, William. *Hamlet*. UK: Penguin Classics ,2015 .Print.

Sharma, Surbhi. "Rethinking of the Status of Goddesses in Indian and Greek Mythology: A Prefatory Comment." *The Achievers Journal: Journal of English Language, Literature and Culture* 6.4 (2021): 14-28. Web. 18 December 2020.

Shreekumar, Sharmila and K.C. Bindu. "Performing Woman, Performing Body: Adapting *Nagamandala for Feminist Theatre*." (eds.) Tutun Mukherjee. *Girish Karnad's Plays Performance and Critical Perspectives*. New Delhi: Penecraft, 2006. Print.

Slotkin, Richard. *Regeneration Through Violence: The Mythology of the American Frontier, 1600-1860*. Connecticut: Wesleyan University, 1973. Print.

Singh, Krishna. "Girish Karnad: A Man and Artist—Evolution of His Dramatic Genius."

The Criterion: An International Journal in English II.III (2011): 11-21. Print.

Singh, Pankaj K. and Jaidev, "Decentring the Patriarchal Myth: Bhisham Sahni's Madhavi," *From Myths to Markets: Essays on Gender*. eds. Kumkum Sangari. NewDelhi: Manohar, 2003. Print.

Somadeva. *Kathasaritsagara (The Ocean of Story)*. Trns. C.H. Tawney. New Delhi: B.R.,2014. Print.

Spivak, G. C. (1988). "Can the Subaltern Speak?" In C. Nelson & L. Grossberg (Eds.), *Marxism and the Interpretation of Culture* (pp. 271-313). University of Illinois Press.

Stevens, Thomas Wood. "How Good Is Eugene O'Neill?" *The English Journal* 26.3 (1937): 179–87. *JSTOR*. 25 May 2022.

Stokely, E. M. *Phantammeron*. US: Giantisland, 2015. Print.

Subramaniam, Savithri. "Myth psychology and reality an in_depth reading of Eugene O Neill s major plays." PhD. Thesis. U of Manonmaniam Sundaranar. 2008. Print.

"The Plays of Aeschylus." *Britannica Encyclopaedia*. Web. 3 Jan 2020. https://www.britannica.com/biography/Aeschylus-Greek-dramatist/The-plays

Tornqvist, Egil. "Personal Nomenclature in the Plays of O'Neill." *Modern Drama* (1966):362-373. Print.

Tynan, Kenneth. *Curtain*. New York: Antheneum, 1961. Print.

Umadevi, A.. "Identity Crisis in Eugene O'Neill's *the Hairy Ape*." *The Criterion: An International Journal in English* 3.3 (2012): 1-11. Web. 29 August 2021.

Winther, Sophus Keith. "Desire Under The Elms: A Modern Tragedy." *Modern Drama*

3.3. (1960): 326-332. Print.

Wordsworth, William. Eds. *Selected Poems*. New Delhi: Penguin Classics, 2004. Print. Yadav, Raju B. "Race and Gender in Yayati." (eds.) Tutun Mukherjee. *Girish Karnad's*

Plays Performance and Critical Perspectives. New Delhi: Penecraft, 2006. Print.

Yadav, Saryug. "Indian English Drama: Tradition and Achievement" *Indian English Drama: Critical Perspectives*. Eds. Dodiya, K. Jaydipsingh and Surendran, K.V. New Delhi: Sarup and Sons, 2002. Print.